ATLAS OF BRITISH HISTORY

OTHER BOOKS BY MARTIN GILBERT

The Churchill biography
Volume III, 'The Challenge of War', 1914–1916
Volume III, Documents, Parts I and II
Volume IV, 'The Stricken World', 1917–1922
Volume IV, Documents, Parts I, II and III
Volume V, 'The Prophet of Truth', 1922–1939
The Exchequer Years, Documents, 1922–1929
The Wilderness Years, Documents, 1929–1935
The Coming of War, Documents, 1936–1939
Volume VI, 'Finest Hour', 1939–1941
At the Admiralty, Documents, 1939–1940
Volume VII, 'Road to Victory', 1941–1945
Volume VIII, 'Never Despair', 1945–1965

Historical works
The Appeasers (with Richard Gott)
The European Powers, 1900–1945
The Roots of Appeasement
Britain and Germany Between the Wars (documents)
Plough My Own Furrow: the Life of Lord Allen of Hurtwood (documents)
Servant of India: Diaries of the Viceroy's Private Secretary (documents)
Sir Horace Rumbold: Portrait of a Diplomat
Churchill: a Photographic Portrait
Churchill's Political Philosophy
Auschwitz and the Allies
Exile and Return: the Struggle for Jewish Statehood
The Jews of Hope: the Plight of Soviet Jewry Today
Shcharansky: Hero of our Time
Jerusalem: Rebirth of a City, 1838–1898
Final Journey: the Fate of the Jews in Nazi Europe
The Holocaust: the Jewish Tragedy
The Second World War
Churchill, A Life

Atlases
Dent Atlas of American History
Dent Atlas of the Arab–Israeli Conflict
Dent Atlas of the First World War
Dent Atlas of the Holocaust
Dent Atlas of Jewish History
Dent Atlas of Recent History (*in preparation*)
Dent Atlas of Russian History
The Jews of Arab Lands: Their History in Maps
The Jews of Russia: Their History in Maps
Jerusalem: Illustrated History Atlas
Children's Illustrated Bible Atlas

ATLAS OF
BRITISH HISTORY

Second edition

Martin Gilbert

Fellow of Merton College, Oxford

New York

OXFORD UNIVERSITY PRESS

1993

© 1968 and 1993 Martin Gilbert

First published in Great Britain by
The Orion Publishing Group Limited
5 Upper St. Martin's Lane, London WC2H 9EA

Published in the United States of America by
Oxford University Press, Inc.
200 Madison Avenue
New York, N.Y. 10016, U.S.A.

Oxford is a registered trademark of
Oxford University Press

Library of Congress
Cataloging-in-Publication Data
Gilbert, Martin, 1936–
    Atlas of British history / Martin Gilbert.
        p.   cm.
    Rev. ed. of: British history atlas / Martin Gilbert. 1969.
    Includes bibliographical references and index.
    ISBN 0–19–521040–9 (hardback)
    ISBN 0–19–521060–3 (paperback)
    1. Great Britain—Historical geography—Maps.   I. Gilbert.
Martin, 1936–   British history atlas.
G1811.SIG5   1993   <G&M>
911. 42—dc20
                                        93–21922
                                           CIP
                                           MAP

Printing (last digit): 9 8 7 6 5 4 3 2

Printed in Great Britain

Preface

The maps in this atlas are intended to provide a visual introduction to British history. I have used the word 'British' in its widest sense, including when relevant England, Scotland, Ireland and Wales, the changing overseas empire, the wars and treaties in which Britain engaged, the alliances in time of peace, the growth of industry and trade, and, on five of the maps, famine and plague.

The story of the British Isles forms the central theme. I have included maps to illustrate economic, social and political problems as well as territorial and military ones. I hope this atlas will help to show that there is more to British history than Hastings and Crécy, Blenheim and Waterloo, Passchendaele and Dunkirk, all of which moments of glory I have tried to put in their wider, and no less important, contexts.

For the maps covering the period before the Norman Conquest the sources are often conflicting on specific details. I have therefore drawn these maps on the basis of probability. In many instances precise knowledge of early frontiers is lacking. I have tried nevertheless to give a clear if also, of necessity, an approximate picture.

As British history advances from wattle huts to timber mansions, and thence on to steel and concrete, so too do the number and variety of facts available to the historian. This is reflected in the maps themselves. I have tried to avoid too complex or too cluttered a page; but a map cannot always satisfy all the demands made upon it, and only the reader can judge where clarity of design and sufficiency of information have been successfully combined.

I am under an obligation of gratitude to those historians and colleagues who kindly scrutinised my draft maps at an early stage, and who made many suggestions for their scope and improvement; in particular Dr J. M. Wallace-Hadrill, Dr Roger Highfield, Mr Ralph Davis, Mr T. F. R. G. Braun, Dr C. C. Davies and Miss Barbara Malament. When the maps were more completed, they were checked by Mr Adrian Scheps, Mr Edmund Ranallo, Mrs Elizabeth Goold, Mr Tony Lawdham and Mrs Jean Kelly, to all of whom my thanks are due.

Twenty-five years have passed since the first edition of this atlas. Within a year of its publication, violence in Northern Ireland re-emerged at the centre of the political stage: I have drawn three new maps to reflect this. The evolution of the European Community has led to growing British participation in Europe, culminating in the Maastricht Treaty of February 1992 and the Edinburgh Summit of December 1992, both of which are a part of the new maps. The Falkland Islands and Persian Gulf wars are included, as are the natural and man-made disasters of the past forty years. Also mapped are many of the problems and challenges of the 1990s, among them asylum, charity, homelessness, unemployment, trade, education, religious diversity, and ethnic minorities. Britain's oil and gas resources are a new feature, as is the most recent phase of the reduction of British overseas possessions, her dwindling military and naval commitments world wide, and her new overseas responsibilities.

The first 118 maps were produced for this atlas by Arthur Banks and his team of cartographers, including Terry Bicknell. The new maps in this edition were produced by Tim Aspden and Robert Bradbrook; I have been helped considerably in the task of compiling them by Abe Eisenstat and Kay Thomson. For their help in providing material for this volume, I would also like to thank the Information Officer, Private Secretary's Office, Buckingham Palace; the Board of Deputies of British Jews, Central Information Desk; the Building Societies Association Press Office; the Lesotho High Commission; the Race Relations Commission; the Refugee Arrivals Project, London Airport; and the Royal Ulster Constabulary Press Office, Belfast.

24 June 1993

MARTIN GILBERT
Merton College, Oxford

Maps

THE CELTS IN BRITAIN BY 50 BC

PICTI

OTADINI

Tweed

SELGOVAE

NOVANTAE

BRIGANTES

Ouse

Trent

DEGEANGLI

CORNOVII

ICENI

ORDOVICES

CORITANI

Welland

Severn

TRINOVANTES

DEMETAE

SILURES

CATUVELLAUNI

Thames

DOBUNI

ATREBATES

CANTII

BELGAE

REGNI

DUROTRIGES

DUMNONII

0   50
Miles

■ Celtic Tribes

1

THE ROMAN CONQUEST 54 BC – 100AD

83 AD. Brought under Roman Control

79 AD. Brought under Roman Control

61 AD. Romans massacre Druids

78 AD. Agricola crosses the Trent

78 AD. Brought under Roman Control

BRIGANTES

York
77

Anglesey

Chester
77

Wroxeter
47

Lincoln
47

ICENI ▨Venta Icenorum

SILURES

Gloucester
50

Caerleon
75

Colchester

CATUVELLAUNI

Verulam

London

ATREBATES

BELGAE

North Downs Trackway

▨Winchester

CANTII

REGNI

GAUL

Legend:

◀ Route of Julius Caesar's expedition 54 BC
▨ Celtic Towns
◀ Roman advances 43-83 AD
░ Celtic Tribes who resisted the Romans
▣ Roman Forts, with date of foundation (all AD)
▓ Caractacus' revolt against the Romans 43 AD
◁ Boadicea's unsuccessful attack on the Romans 61 AD

0 ——— 50
Miles

ROMAN MILITARY GOVERNMENT 100 AD–400 AD

Antonine Wall

Hadrian's Wall

VI Legion
York

Military Capital

Chester
XX Legion

Ermine Street

Fosse Way

Watling Street

II Legion
Caerleon

London

Fosse Way

Military Government
Headquarters of Legions
Fortresses and military camps
Roman roads
Celtic trackways used by Romans
Coastal forts 300–400 A D
These were controlled by
the Count of the Saxon Shore

0   50
Miles

CIVILIAN LIFE IN ROMAN BRITAIN

Hadrian's Wall

Carlisle
LEAD
COAL

COPPER
COAL

Darlington

LEAD
SILVER
IRON

York

COAL

COAL

Manchester

Lincoln
Horncastle

LEAD

COPPER

SILVER
LEAD

SILVER

Newark
Ancaster

COPPER
Lichfield
Wroxeter
LEAD

Leicester

Castor

Caistor

Worcester

Cambridge

Towcester

Colchester

TIN
Kenchester

Alchester

GOLD

Gloucester

Dorchester
St. Albans

IRON
COAL
Cirencester
Caerwent

LEAD

Bath

Mildenhall

London
Rochester
Canterbury

Silchester

COAL

IRON

IRON

LEAD

Winchester

STONE

Bitterne
Chichester

STONE

Exeter

Dorchester

TIN

TIN

	Civilian Government
	Main wheat-growing areas
	Mines and quarries
	Potteries
	Regional capitals
	Other towns

0   50
Miles

THE PATTERN OF ROMAN SETTLEMENT IN SOUTHERN ENGLAND

Cold Kitchen Hill

Temple

Old Sarum

stone quarries

Villas

Villa

Sherborne
Villa

Villa

Villa

Hod Hill Fort

Villa

Villa

Badbury

Aqueduct

Dorchester

Temple

Temple

Villa

stone quarries

Land over 250 feet

Celtic fields still tilled in Roman times

⊙ Farms

✪ Towns

△ Pottery kilns

━ Principal Roman roads

0   8
Miles

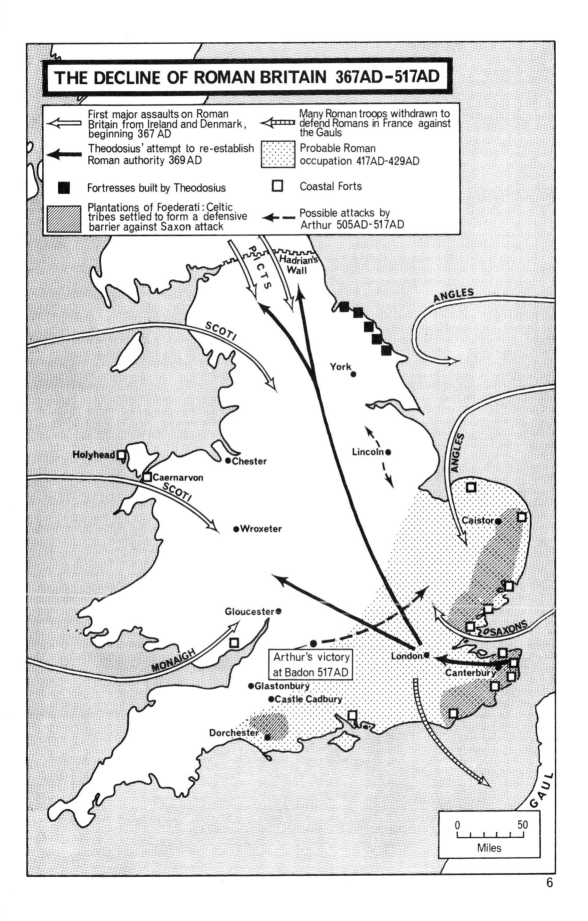

THE DECLINE OF ROMAN BRITAIN 367AD–517AD

First major assaults on Roman Britain from Ireland and Denmark, beginning 367 AD

Theodosius' attempt to re-establish Roman authority 369 AD

Fortresses built by Theodosius

Plantations of Foederati: Celtic tribes settled to form a defensive barrier against Saxon attack

Many Roman troops withdrawn to defend Romans in France against the Gauls

Probable Roman occupation 417AD–429AD

Coastal Forts

Possible attacks by Arthur 505AD–517AD

PICTS

Hadrian's Wall

ANGLES

SCOTI

York

ANGLES

Holyhead

Chester

Lincoln

Caernarvon

SCOTI

Caistor

Wroxeter

Gloucester

London

SAXONS

MONAIGH

Canterbury

Arthur's victory at Badon 517AD

Glastonbury

Castle Cadbury

Dorchester

GAUL

0   50

Miles

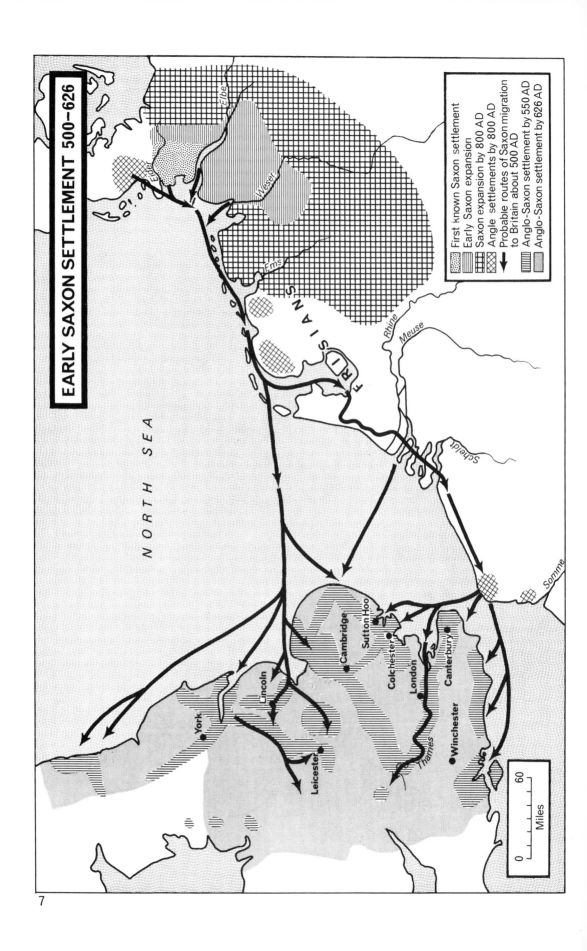

EARLY SAXON SETTLEMENT 500–626

First known Saxon settlement
Early Saxon expansion
Saxon expansion by 800 AD
Angle settlements by 800 AD
Probable routes of Saxon migration
to Britain about 500 AD
Anglo-Saxon settlement by 550 AD
Anglo-Saxon settlement by 626 AD

NORTH SEA

F R I S I A N S

Elbe
Eider
Weser
Ems
Rhine
Meuse
Scheldt
Somme

York
Lincoln
Leicester
Cambridge
Sutton Hoo
Colchester
London
Canterbury
Winchester
Thames

0   60
Miles

SAXON KINGDOMS AND BRETWALDASHIPS 630-829

EGBERT 802-829

CELTS

NORTHUMBRIA

LINDSEY

MERCIA

EAST ANGLIA

KENT

WESSEX

CELTS

CELTS

■ Kingdom of Egbert
First "King of the English"

Bretwaldaship (overkingship) of Egbert

OFFA 757-796

NORTHUMBRIA

CELTS

LINDSEY

MERCIA

EAST ANGLIA

ESSEX

KENT

SUSSEX

WESSEX

CELTS

CELTS

0   50
Miles

■ Kingdom of Offa

Bretwaldaship (overkingship) of Offa

EDWIN 630

BERNICIA NORTHUMBRIA DEIRA

CELTS

LINDSEY

MERCIA

ESSEX

KENT

WESSEX

CELTS UNDER GWYNEDD

CELTS

ISLE OF MAN

ANGLESEY

■ Kingdom of Edwin

Bretwaldaship (overkingship) of Edwin

8

THE CHURCH 700–850

† Abercorn
Coldingham ✛
Lindisfarne
† Melrose
🏴 Coquet Island

LINDISFARNE

WHITHORN
† Whithorn

Hexham † † Tynemouth
† Jarrow
† Monkwearmouth
HEXHAM
Hartlepool ✛
†Gainford
Gilling ⚡ †Sockburn Whitby
Lastingham †
Hackness †
† Ripon
†York

Y O R K

† Barrow
Syddensis Civitas
(site not known)

LINDSEY

LICHFIELD

Elmham
ELMHAM

Repton ✛ † Breedon
Lichfield
Peterborough †
Leicester †Oundle Ely ✛
Dunwich
† Brixworth † Bury St.
LEICESTER Edmunds
DUNWICH

HEREFORD
Worcester
WORCESTER
Hereford

DORCHESTER
LONDON
† Malmesbury
Abingdon Dorchester ✛ Barking
London Reculver
ROCH- Minster
ESTER
WINCHESTER † Woking Canterbury Dover
Glastonbury † Winchester **CANTER-** Folkestone
Sherborne †Tisbury **SELSEY BURY** Lyminge
Nursling † Selsey
SHERBORNE Wimborne† Selsey
Exeter †

Legend:
† Religious houses founded by 850
✛ Double houses where monks and nuns lived under the rule of an abbess
— Approximate diocesan boundaries
● Diocesan seats
▨ Archbishoprics.

0 ——— 50
Miles

VIKING EXPANSION IN EUROPE 700–941

The Viking homeland.

↑ Viking attacks with dates.

Viking settlements by 941.

Viking raids.

CAUCASUS

Trebizond

BLACK SEA

Constantinople

866

Volga

Dniepel

Kiev
882

Ladoga
820

Novgorod

CARPATHIANS

Danube

Vistula

ALPS

MEDITERRANEAN SEA

Birka

SWEDES

Trelleborg

DANES

Hedeby

Genoa

888

Marseilles

Trondheim

NORSE

Rouen

859

Loire

800

843 862 847

843

903

FAROE IS.

700

SHETLAND IS.

ORKNEY IS.

703

874

ICELAND

Reykjavik

B

10

THE NORSE AND DANISH INVASIONS 793-876

NORSE

NORSE

NORSE

NORSE

NORSE
Sacked 793 A.D.
Lindisfarne

798 A.D.

Luel
Jarrow
Wearmouth

York

DANES
RAGNAR
LOTHBROK
860 A.D.
841 A.D.

Torksey

IRELAND
853 Norse
kingdom founded
Dublin

Nottingham
Repton

Thetford
Cambridge

870 A.D.

NORSE

853 A.D.

793 A.D.

841 A.D.

834-
876 A.D.

Ashdown
London
Reading

834-
876 A.D.

NORSE
793-850 A.D.

Basing

Wilton

WELAND 860 A.D.
840 A.D.

840 A.D.

800 A.D.

868 A.D.

DANES

DANES

Viking raids, with dates.

Viking rule by 876.

Viking overlordship by 876.

Winter quarters of the
Great Danish Army.

Main battles between
Danes and Saxons.

0   50

Miles

Wessex 876

Danish attacks 876

Danish campaigns 877-878

Danish base camps 876-878

Boundary between the Danelaw and
the English kingdoms of Mercia and
Wessex, established by Treaty 886

Fortified towns in Wessex 890

Reconquered from the Danes 912-918

0   50

Miles

S C O T L A N D

STRATHCLYDE

GALLOWAY

NORTHUMBRIA

THE NORSE
KINGDOM
OF YORK

○ York

Edward the Elder receives the
submission of the King of the
Scots, the Norse ruler of York
and the people of Northumbria

918

917
○
Bakewell

DANISH

MERCIA

918

ENGLISH

MERCIA

GUTHRUM'S KINGDOM

917

■ Cambridge

914

Gloucester ■

Danes defeated
by Alfred 878

912

Reading ■

London

Chippenham

Alfred's base camp 878

Edington

W E S S E X

Athelney ○

Wareham

Exeter ■

THE ENGLISH RESURGENCE 876-920

THE ENGLISH RESURGENCE 920–973

NORSE

STRATHCLYDE

LOTHIAN

NORTHUMBRIA

GALLOWAY

Isle of Man

York

Manchester

Thelwall

Dublin

Runcorn

Chester

Eddisbury

EAST ANGLIA

MERCIA

Brunanburgh
(site unknown)

937 Norse invasion repulsed by combined forces of Wessex and Mercia.

Bath

KENT

WESSEX

931 Athelstan sets up an English bishopric.

973. Coronation of Edgar. With the triple act of crowning, anointing, and a coronation oath, the continuous history of the English coronation service began.

	Norse conquests 900–920
	Northern limit of English rule in 920
	Northern limit of English rule in 927
←	Athelstan's attack on Scotland 934
	Ceded to the Scots by Edgar 975
⊕	English fortified towns

0   50
Miles

THE DANISH EMPIRE 1000-1034

Legend:
- The Danish Kingdom in 1000
- Burnt by Danes 1010
- Archbishop murdered by Danes 1012
- Surrendered to Danes under Swein Forkbeard 1013
- Edmund Ironside defeated by Canute 1016
- Canute's conquests by 1016
- Canute's expeditions 1023-1028
- Danish conquests by 1034
- English missionary churches

THE DANISH KINGS OF ENGLAND

CANUTE
1016-1035

HAROLD HAREFOOT
1035-1040

HARTHACANUTE
1040-1042

Trondheim

TRONDELAG

ROGALAND

Stavanger

SMALAND

DENMARK

Ribe

1033 Granted to Canute by the Pope

ENGLAND

Oxford   Ashingdon

Winchester   London
Canterbury

1027 Canute's pilgrimage to Rome

On Harthacanute's death the throne of England reverted to an Englishman, Edward the Confessor.

0   200
Miles

BISHOPRICS AND MONASTERIES 1000-1066

ST. CUTHBERT'S SEE

Chester-le-Street
Carlisle
Durham

Y O R K
York

Barton-on-Humber

Lincoln

LICHFIELD
Lichfield

North Elmham
St Benet of Hulme
E L M H A M
Ramsey
Ely
Bury St.Edmunds

HEREFORD
Worcester
Hereford

D O R C H E S T E R

WORCESTER
Westbury on Trym
Abingdon
Dorchester
LONDON
London

Ramsbury
RAMSBURY
Ramsbury

CANTERBURY
Rochester
Canterbury

Wells
WINCHESTER
Winchester

Dover

WELLS
Sherborne

SELSEY
Selsey   Sompting
ROCHESTER

CREDITON
Exeter
SHERBORNE
Crediton

ST. GERMANS

1058 joins with Ramsbury

1027 Sees join

Boundaries of the bishoprics
✠ Cathedral minsters
✠ Cathedral monasteries
● Monasteries

0   50
Miles

HAROLD'S DEFEAT 1066

5 September 1066. Harold Hardrada joined Tostig from Norway. They moved south, raiding along the coast and reached York

7 25 September 1066. Harold defeated Norse army. Harold Hardrada and Tostig both killed

Raids on coast

Stamford Bridge

York

LINDSEA

3 June 1066. Tostig defeated by Earl Edwin and Lindsea militia. His invasion repulsed, he retreated to Scotland

2 May 1066. Tostig landed again and ravaged countryside

190 Miles

6 September 1066. Harold marched north to halt invasion

9 14 October 1066. Having marched from York, Harold was defeated and killed at Hastings

London

60 Miles

Sandwich

1 May 1066. Sandwich attacked and occupied by Harold's brother Tostig, who withdrew when attacked by Harold's militia

4 August 1066. Harold disbanded militia and dispersed his fleet as danger seemed over

Hastings

8 28 September 1066. William of Normandy landed

0   40
Miles

◁— Norse fleet
◀— Harold's campaigns
◁— Norman fleet

THE NORMAN CONQUEST 1066–1072

1070 King Malcolm of Scotland invades
1072 Malcolm acknowledges William's suzerainty

SCOTLAND

Jarrow

1070

York

1070

1068

Chester

1069

Lincoln

1068

Nottingham

1069

Stafford

1070

Shrewsbury

Norwich

Ely

Warwick

Huntingdon

Cambridge

Ipswich

Wallingford

London

Sandwich

1068

Canterbury
Dover

1067

Winchester

Salisbury

Hastings

Exeter

0   50
Miles

William's campaign 1066
Subsequent Norman
campaigns with dates
Saxon risings before 1072
King Swein of Denmark
invades, but repulsed 1069

ENGLAND UNDER THE NORMANS 1066–1100

NORMAN KINGS OF ENGLAND
William The Conqueror 1066–1087
William Rufus 1087–1100
Henry I 1100–1135

DURHAM

Carlisle

1093 Durham Cathedral

York

Fulford

Lincoln

CHESTER

SHREWSBURY

Stamford

1096
Norwich Cathedral Nave

1083
Ely Cathedral

Huntingdon

Cambridge

HEREFORD

1089 Gloucester
Abbey Church

1077
St. Albans Abbey

Monmouth
Caerleon

Oxford

Wallingford

London

Westminster Hall
1097

KENT

Canterbury Cathedral Crypt 1096

Winchester Cathedral
1079

Dover

Sherborne

Southampton

Exeter

Carisbrooke

Tintagel

Corfe

The Marcher Earldoms

Area covered by Domesday
Book volume I, 1086

Area covered by Domesday
Book volume II, 1086

Royal castles

Baronial castles

Religious buildings begun

0   50
Miles

THE NORMAN CONQUEST OF WALES 1068-1200

Earl of Chester

Fitzalan

Corbet

Earl of Hereford

Marshall

Lacy

Mortimer

Braose

G W Y N E D D

P O W Y S

DEHEUBARTH

Fitzmartin

0 10
Miles

Welsh Kingdoms
GWYNEDD
POWYS
DEHEUBARTH

Norman advances 1068
Norman advances 1100
Occupied by Anglo-Norman Marcher barons by 1200
Anglo-Norman Marcher families
Norman Castles built by 1200

20

NORMAN RULE 1066-1087

FLANDERS

BURGUNDY

Paris

ENGLAND

York

London

N O R M A N D Y

ANJOU

POITOU

B R I T T A N Y

M A I N E

0 100
Miles

Territory directly ruled by William of Normandy
French dependency of William
Possessions of the King of France

19

ANGLO-FRANCE 1189

HOLY ROMAN EMPIRE

BURGUNDY

Calais
Gisors
Paris
Rouen
NORMANDY
Château Gaillard
Caen
MAINE
Le Mans
Angers
ANJOU
Chinon
Poitiers
POITOU
AQUITAINE
Bordeaux
GUYENNE
GASCONY
TOULOUSE
Toulouse
Nîmes
BRITTANY
NAVARRE
ARAGON

	Possessions of Henry II
	Dependencies of Henry II
	Possessions of the King of France
	Dependencies of the King of France

0   100
Miles

22

IRELAND 1150

0   50
Miles

ULSTER
O'Neill
De Courcy
O'Carroll
O'Rourke
O'Connor
CONNAUGHT
O'Dowd
O'Flaherty
O'Kelly
O'Shaughnessy
MEATH
Annaly
De Lacy
Offaly
O'Dempsey
LEINSTER
De Clare
MacMurrough
McGillipatrick
Thomond
Ormond
MUNSTER
McCarthy
Desmond
O'Sullivan
Decies

	Scottish settlement areas
	Boundaries of the Five Kingdoms
	Norman families
	Irish clans

21

THE CHURCH 1100-1300

The Cistercians stressed manual labour and fieldwork. They introduced many farming improvements and were large exporters of wool. By 1200 there were over 100 Cistercian houses in England.

Rievaulx
Byland
Ripon Cathedral 1154
Furness
Fountains
York Minster Nave 1291

Lincoln Cathedral 1185

Lichfield Cathedral 1280

Tintern

Canterbury Cathedral Choir 1174

Wells Cathedral Nave 1214
Salisbury Cathedral 1220

✝ Cistercian foundations 1127–1180
⊕ Cistercian foundations 1180–1300
✪ Houses of the Dominican friars 1221–1300
◕ Houses of the Franciscan friars 1230–1300
♣ Other religious buildings begun

0   50
Miles

STEPHEN AND MATILDA
1135-1148

Legend:

▣ Towns and castles loyal to Stephen nephew of Henry I

▨ Main sphere of influence of Matilda daughter of Henry I

▤ Land controlled by Matilda's half-brother Robert of Gloucester

▥ Land controlled by Geoffrey de Mandeville 1140-43

0 _____ 100

Miles

SCOTLAND

④ Rebellion of Rannulf of Chester. Stephen defeated at Lincoln and taken to Winchester where Matilda is elected Domina Anglorum April 1141.

■ York

⑨ 1143-4 Ravaged by Geoffrey de Mandeville. Religious houses plundered. Towns burned. Citizens tortured. De Mandeville dies 1144.

Lincoln ●

● Chester

③ 1136-8 Stephen suppresses rebellions

N O R F O L K

Ely ●

● Cambridge

WALES

⑦ 1142 Captured and burnt by Stephen. Matilda escapes to Wallingford.

Colchester ■ ▪ Ramsey

Gloucester ●

● Oxford

① 1135 Towns refuse to admit Stephen on his arrival in England

● Faringdon

● Wallingford

London ■

⑩ 1145 Stephen cuts off Robert of Gloucester from Matilda (then at Wallingford). Two years later Robert dies. In 1148 Matilda flees to France.

② 1135 Stephen elected king

Wilton ●

● Winchester

Canterbury ▪ Dover ●

DEVON

⑤ Feb.-Sept. 1141 Stephen imprisoned. Matilda expelled September. Robert of Gloucester captured. Stephen released

Wareham ▪

■ Boulogne

⑥ 1142 Captured by Stephen. Angevin port for France. Lost in 1143.

⑧ 1143 Stephen is defeated. Robert of Gloucester controls western England.

● Rouen

NORMANDY

ENGLAND 1200–1300

IMPORTANT BOOKS
1193 Gesta Ricardi I
1201 Chronica of Roger of Hoveden
1212 Otia Imperialia
1222 Saxon Law–Code
1250 The Harrowing of Hell
(earliest existing English play)
1266 Opus Maius
1274 De Antiquis Legibus Liber

York

Sherwood
Forest

Shrewsbury
1283

Nottingham

Merton 1264
Balliol 1268
Worcester 1289

Huntingdon
Peterhouse 1284
Cambridge

1278
Gloucester

St. Albans
Council 1213

Epping
Forest

Forest
of
Dean

Provisions of
Oxford 1258

Marlborough
1267

1259
Provisions of
Westminster
1270–72, 1274–86

New
Forest

Winchester

0   50
Miles

■ Royal Forests
✠ Principal Parliaments
● University Foundations

25

THE ECONOMY 1200–1300

1245 Papal money-raiser expelled from England by king, clergy and barons
1274 Anglo-Flanders Commercial Treaty
1275 King to receive duty on wool
1280 German merchants in England form a Hansa
1290 Expulsion of the Jews from England
1299 Act to repress bad coinage passed

York
blues
Beverley

Lincoln scarlets
Lincoln

Nottingham
Stamfords
Norwich

Leicester
Stamford

Somersham
Coventry
Huntingdon
Ramsey
Northampton
Bury St.Edmunds
Worcester
Cambridge
Warwick
Ipswich
Bedford
Sudbury
Gloucester
russets
russets
Colchester
Oxford
russets
Chepstow
Wallingford
London
Bristol
Marlborough
Canterbury
Sandwich
Devizes
Hythe
Dover
russets
Romney
Wilton
Winchester
Rye
Salisbury
Winchelsea
Hastings

Cloth producing areas with names of cloth
Towns with weavers guilds by 1200
The Cinque Ports: special liberties granted 1278
The liberties of Chepstow, Ramsey and Somersham
Towns with Jewish settlements where Jewish loans were recorded 1190–1290

0   50
Miles

26

LONDON 1200–1400

Jewish Quarter. The Jews were expelled in 1290.

1260. House of Friars of the Sac.

Priory of the Minoresses

Royal apartments, mint and armouries.

Tower of London

1253. House of Austin Friars

Guildhall

London Bridge

Rebuilt 1176–1209

Charterhouse

Smithfield

St. Paul's

Steelyard

1272. House of Blackfriars.

Chapel of St. Thomas of Canterbury

Tabard's Inn

The chief magistrate of London was known as the Lord Mayor from 1354.

Fleet Prison

Bridewell

King's Wardrobe

Baynard Castle

The Temple

1224. House of Greyfriars.

1241. House of Whitefriars.

Savoy Palace

1259. Parliament meets

THAMES

WESTMINSTER

To reduce the hazard of fire, special privileges were given to citizens who built their houses in stone.
In 1212 roofing in reeds or straw was forbidden. Tiles, boards or lead had to be used.

Probable population in 1390 : 35,000

Built-up area

City wall, on line of old Roman wall

Private houses belonging to nobles

Foreign merchant communities

Scotland Yard

Whitehall

Westminster Hall

Westminster Abbey

0   ½
    Mile

SCOTLAND 1295–1402

0   30
Miles

1346 Edward III's
Queen Philippa
defeats David II

1402 Percys of
Northumberland
defeat Scots

1318 Captured by
Robert Bruce

1296 Edward I
defeats Scots

1298 Edward I
defeats Wallace

Neville's Cross
Durham

Homildon Hill

Halidon Hill

Dunbar

Berwick

Kelehon

Roxburgh

Kincardine

Dundee

Crail

Scone

Perth

Kinclaven

Edinburgh

Falkirk

Stirling

Tweed

1304 Captured
by Edward I

1297 Scots defeat English

1314 Robert Bruce
defeats Edward II

1333 English victory

1311-1326 Scots ravage
Northern England

Tay

Forth

Bannockburn

Dumbarton

Clyde

Ayr

Rothesay

Kirkcudbright

Wigtown

Tarbert

ENGLAND

Franchise of Tynedale(held by
King of Scotland until 1295)

Disputed land

Franchise of the Bishopric
of Durham

Scottish royal castles

English castles

Scottish victories

English victories

c

28

THE HUNDRED YEARS' WAR 1259-1368

0   100
Miles

Calais
Etaples
Crécy
Abbeville

HOLY

Barfleur
Rouen

ROMAN

Caen
NORMANDY
Paris

Bretigny

EMPIRE

F
R
A
N
C
E

ANJOU   Tours
Bourges
Poitiers
POITOU

DAUPHINÉ

AQUITAINE
Bordeaux
GUYENNE
QUERCY
ROUERGUE

GASCONY
Bayonne
Toulouse

Vitoria
Narbonne

Pass of
Roncesvalles
To Burgos
Pamplona
NAVARRE

ARAGON

■ Possessions of Henry III, 1259	⇨ Edward III's campaign 1346-1349
▫ Possessions of the King of France, 1259	the three campaigns of Edward the Black Prince:
▨ English gains 1275	→ to Narbonne 1355
▩ English gains at the Treaty of Bretigny, 1368	→ to Poitiers 1356
	→ to Burgos 1367

THE CONQUEST OF WALES 1277-1295

5 December 1294
Edward leaves
Chester

Deganwy
Rhuddlan
Conway
Flint
Chester
Bangor
Denbigh
Caernarvon
Derwen
Wrexham
Dolwyddelan
Criccieth
Chirk
Harlech
Oswestry
Shrewsbury
Welshpool
Montgomery
Llanbadarn
Builth
Painscastle
Bronllys
Cardigan
Llywel
Brecon
Carmarthen
Dryslwyn
Merthyr

14 June 1295 Edward
reaches Merthyr

■ Castles   taken by the English 1277-1283
◪ Castles held by the English 1277-1283
⣿ Crown Lordships 1276
▨ Conquered by 1283
← Edward's march through Wales 1294-1295

0   10   20
Miles

30

ENGLAND 1300–1400

The Publication in 1362 of William Langland's PIERS PLOWMAN saw beginning of the use of English instead of French in literature, the law courts and parliament. Chaucer's CANTERBURY TALES were written between 1387 and 1400.

Newcastle

Hartlepool

Ripon

York

Halifax

Hull

Clare 1326
Pembroke 1346
Gonville 1346
Trinity Hall 1350
Corpus Christi 1352

Boston

Exeter 1314
Oriel 1326
Queen's 1340
New 1379

Lynn

Yarmouth

Coventry

Cambridge

Hadleigh Ipswich
Sudbury
Coggeshall
Colchester

Haverfordwest

Northleach

Oxford

London

Bristol

Reading

Sandwich

Bridgwater

1382 Winchester
College founded

Salisbury

Winchester

Chichester

Southampton

Exeter

1366 Parliament refuses to
pay feudal tribute to the Pope

//// Main wool growing areas
..... Fullers Earth deposits: essential
       for absorbing the grease in wool
◉ Centres of the wool industry
■ Ports with substantial export activity
✤ University foundations

0   50
Miles

31

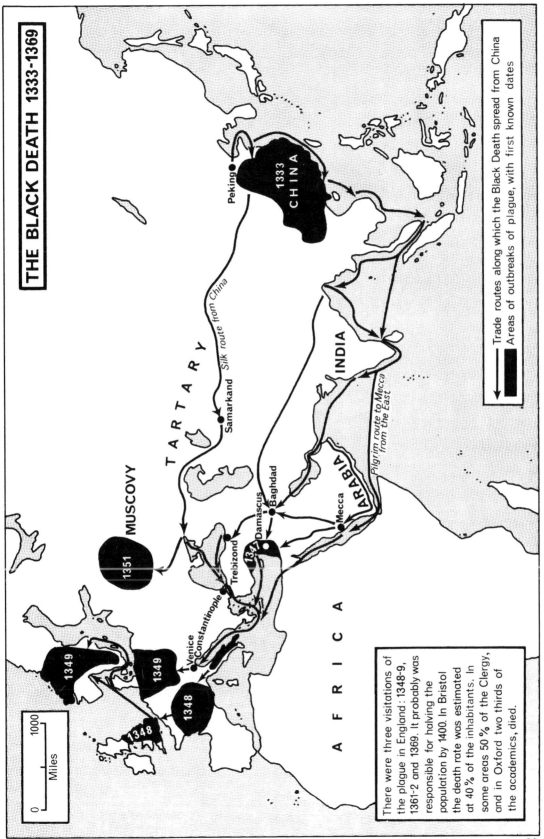

THE BLACK DEATH 1333-1369

Trade routes along which the Black Death spread from China

Areas of outbreaks of plague, with first known dates

CHINA 1333

Peking

TARTARY

Silk route from China

Samarkand

MUSCOVY 1351

INDIA

Baghdad

Damascus 1347

Trebizond

Constantinople

Venice 1349

1349

1348

1348

Mecca

ARABIA

Pilgrim route to Mecca from the East

AFRICA

0 1000
Miles

There were three visitations of the plague in England: 1348-9, 1361-2 and 1369. It probably was responsible for halving the population by 1400. In Bristol the death rate was estimated at 40 % of the inhabitants. In some areas 50 % of the Clergy, and in Oxford two thirds of the academics, died.

THE PEASANTS' REVOLT 1381

Leicester

Norwich

Yarmouth

Mildenhall

Bury St. Edmunds

Cambridge

Ipswich

Sudbury

Dunstable

Colchester

Jack Straw leads peasants into London from the north

St. Albans

Harrow
Hendon
Highbury

Billericay
Brentwood

Mile End

London
Chiswick

Windsor

Twickenham
Croydon

Dartford

Rochester

Richard II leaves for London and receives peasant petition at Mile End. He grants it on 14 June. Nine days later he withdraws his grant and says: "Villeins ye are and villeins ye shall remain." But as a result of the revolt the Poll Tax was abolished.

Winchester

Maidstone

Canterbury

Wat Tyler chosen leader of the revolt

John Ball, a vagrant priest joins revolt

☐ Widespread peasant violence against clergy, tax-collectors and landed gentry.

← Main peasant marches.

⊙ Towns where severe rioting took place. Peasants demanded abolition of villeinage and of the poll tax. Artisans joined the rising to attack burgesses' monopolies and privileges. The lower clergy also supported anti-clerical activity.

0   30
Miles

ENGLAND 1400–1500

Legend:

- ⊞ Cloth producing areas.
- ← Principal ports with exports.
- ⊙ Mines.
- ▨ Areas of relatively small population.
- ◎ Important trade fairs.
- ⊘ Glass making towns.
- ◉ Towns with merchants' houses of size and comfort.
- ⬅ Deep sea fishing fleets which spent all summer in the northern seas, bringing back hake, pollack and salmon.
- ⇐ Principal imports.
- ✳ Riots against Italian merchants accused of dominating wool trade.
- ⊜ University foundations.
- ✂ School Foundation
- △ Jack Cade's rebellion. Middle class revolt against oppressive officials, especially members of the royal household and magnates abusing their power.
- ◓ Major private castles.
- ▲ Early borough incorporations, giving the citizens power by charter to hold land and to issue by-laws in the name of the town. County officials became barred from the town, whose own freely elected officials regulated town life.

coal
Newcastle
1400
▲ COAL

▲ Carlisle
1401
⊙ LEAD

Hull
1440 ▲

King's College 1441
Queens' College 1447
St. Catherine's College 1475
Jesus College 1497

⊙ COAL
⊙ IRON
⊙ IRON

⊙ COAL

Lincoln ▲
1409

Tattershall ◉ wool

⊙ COAL ⊙ LEAD 1448 ▲
Nottingham

Boston
wool grain
Lynn

Blakeney
Cromer

Caister

Rugeley ⊘

Norwich ◉ ▲
1417

Stourbridge ◎

Northampton

Cambridge ⊘

wool, cloth, tin, lead, hides, calfskin

1483. Royal College of Arms established.

1407. Parliament upholds right of the Commons to originate all money grants, thus consolidating its political power.

Gloucester △

Woodstock ▲ 1453
◎⊜ Oxford

wool, tin, cloth

1476. Caxton establishes printing press.

⊙ COAL
lead cloth
Bristol
⊙ LEAD

Eton ✂ 1441
Westminster
1456, 1457

London

△ 1450
Sandwich

Lincoln College 1427
All Souls' 1437
Magdalen 1485
Duke Humphrey's Library 1488

IRON ⊙ IRON ⊙ IRON
Chiddingfold

Hurstmonceux ◓

Winchester ◎
1460

wool, cloth, tin, lead, hides, calfskin

✳ ● Southampton
1445 ▲

⊙ TIN

⊙ TIN
⊙ TIN ⊙ LEAD
▲ Plymouth
1439
⊙ TIN

MAJOR IMPORTS

Fine armour, spices, drugs, rhubarb, oriental silks, cotton, sweet wines, currants, sugar, velvets, satins, precious stones, gold and silver ware, parchment, writing paper, blue dye.

THE DEFEAT OF OWEN GLENDOWER 1405-1412

36

Territory recovered
from Glendower

- 1406-1407
- 1407-1409
- 1410-1412

- – – Campaign of the Welsh in 1405
- —— Campaign of the English in 1405
- ☐ Castles besieged by the Welsh
- ■ Castles besieged by the English

Harlech
Llanbadarn
Carmarthen
Coity
Tenby 1405
Haverfordwest

1405

Wye
Usk
Towy
Dee
Severn

0   40
Miles

OWEN GLENDOWER'S REVOLT 1400 – 1405

35

Territory held
by Glendower

- 1400
- 1401
- 1402
- 1403-1405

- – – Campaigns of the Welsh with dates
- —— Campaigns of the English with dates
- ☐ Castles besieged by the Welsh
- ■ Castles besieged by the English

Flint
Hawarden
Holt
Shrewsbury
Rhuddlan
Denbigh
Ruthin 1400
Oswestry
1402
Welshpool
Caernarvon
1400 and 1402
1400
Brecon
1404
Carmarthen
1401
1401
1403
Usk
Abergavenny
Caerleon
Newport
1402
Cardiff
1403
1403

1401
1403

0   40
Miles

THE COLLAPSE OF ENGLISH RULE IN FRANCE 1429-1453

1431 Joan of Arc burnt at the stake.

HOLY

ROMAN

EMPIRE

Calais

Harfleur
Rouen
Compiègne
Reims
Caen
Bayeux
Fourmigny
Paris
Châlons-sur-Marne
Verneuil
Montlhery
BRITTANY
Patay
Rouvray
Troyes
Le Mans
Orléans
MAINE

BURGUNDY

POITOU

1429 Joan of Arc enters Orléans and defeats the English at Patay.

SAVOY

F R A N C E

Cognac

Bourg
Bordeaux
Castillon

Avignon

PROVENCE

English possessions in France 1429.

Burgundy, allied with England.

French possessions and dependencies.

Papal territory.

English towns besieged or sacked by France.

French victories.

Last remaining English possession in France 1453.

0   100
Miles

THE WARS OF THE ROSES: TERRITORIAL DIVISIONS 1450

Chief areas of Lancastrian influence (including Neville and Percy)

Chief areas of Yorkist influence

Manors and lands of the Duke of Clarence

Crown lands (Lancastrian control)

0   50
Miles

ENGLISH TRADING COMPANIES 1467-1696

MUSCOVY COMPANY 1554

LEVANT COMPANY 1592

EAST INDIA COMPANY 1600

EASTLAND COMPANY 1579

MERCHANT ADVENTURERS 1467

MOROCCO COMPANY 1595

GUINEA COMPANY 1588

HUDSON BAY COMPANY 1670

PLYMOUTH COMPANY 1696

LONDON COMPANY 1606

Principal trade marts

Hinterland trading areas

IRELAND 1500-1558

ULSTER

Belfast

Dundalk

Drogheda

Dublin

Wicklow

Wexford

Carrick

CONNAUGHT

Limerick

KERRY

Cork

Kinsale

0   50
Miles

The Pale of English settlement

Added to the Pale by Henry VII

Scottish immigration

WALES 1500-1535

Denbigh

D E N B I G H

Bangor

Caernarvon

MONTGOMERY

Montgomery

RADNOR

Radnor

Cardigan

Carmarthen

Brecon

BRECKNOCK

Monmouth

MONMOUTH

GLAMORGAN

Cardiff

PEMBROKE

Pembroke

The shires were established
by the Act of Union of 1536

Crown Lands in 1500

Principal towns

0   20
Miles

THE PATTERN OF MONASTIC PROPERTY 1500–1530

BISHOPRIC OF LONDON

BISHOPRIC OF ROCHESTER

BISHOPRIC OF WINCHESTER

BISHOPRIC OF LINCOLN

BISHOPRIC OF SALISBURY

LONDON

Saffron Walden

Ware

Waltham

St Albans

Woburn

Westminster

Southwark

Rochester

Darfford

Waverley

Windsor

Reading

Dorchester

Oxford

Wallingford

Abingdon

Newbury

Legend:
Important monasteries (with an income of over £200 or at least 16 monks)
Houses of regular canons
Smaller religious houses of all kinds
Houses of friars
Areas of special religious jurisdiction
Boundaries of the bishoprics

0   10
Miles

THE ENGLISH REFORMATION 1531–1571

0   50
Miles

1531 Henry VIII recognized as supreme head of the English Church by Parliament
1533 The Pope excommunicates Henry VIII.
1534 Act of Supremacy. Church of England severed itself from Rome.
1535 Sir Thomas More beheaded. Canonised in 1935.
1536 Dissolution of monasteries begun.
1539 Henry VIII issues Six Articles: repealed 1547.
1549 First Act of Uniformity. First Prayer Book.
1552 Second Act of Uniformity. Second Prayer Book.
1554 Reconciliation with Rome under Queen Mary. Roman Catholicism restored.
1559 Queen Elizabeth reintroduced the Act of Supremacy. Catholicism ceased to be the religion of England.
1571 Parliament forbids the import of Papal Bulls into England.

Carlisle

Jervaulx
Bridlington
Fountains
York
Whalley
Pontefract
CHESTER
Doncaster
Louth
Barling
Lincoln
Kirkstead
Lenton

PETERBOROUGH

OXFORD

Woburn
Colchester

GLOUCESTER

Bishops Ridley and Latimer burnt by Catholics in 1555

Oxford
London
Canterbury
Reading

BRISTOL
Glastonbury

Becket's shrine destroyed by protestants in 1538

Areas affected by the Pilgrimage of Grace 1536-1537
Monasteries whose abbots were executed by Henry VIII.
Bishoprics created by Henry VIII

44

SCOTLAND 1500–1603

Legend:
- Universities with dates of foundation
- Lands of Highland clans who remained Catholic
- Lands where Lutheran teaching spread quickly
- Area of influence of Northern Earls who rose in support of Mary, 1569
- Battles from Flodden (1513) to Langside (1568)

In 1603 King James VI of Scotland became King James I of England

1559. John Knox preaching reformed Christianity

1544. Sacked by English

1547. English victory in attempt at union

1567. Successful Protestant rising

1513. James IV killed. English repulse the Scottish invasion

1547. James V killed. English repulse the Scottish attack

1568. Defeat of Mary Queen of Scots, who fled to England

Dingwall

Elgin

Aberdeen 1494

Dundee

Perth

1410 St. Andrews Crail

Stirling

Glasgow 1451 1583 Pinkie
Langside Edinburgh Carberry Hill

Wigtown Kirkudbright

Solway Moss

Flodden

ENGLAND

Loch Ness Spey Tay Firth of Forth Clyde Tweed Tyne Tees

0   50
Miles

45

ENGLAND 1500-1600

Land enclosed before 1500
Widespread enclosure 1500-1600
Some enclosure 1500-1600
University foundations
School foundations

OXFORD
Brasenose 1509
Corpus Christi 1516
Christ Church 1546
Trinity 1554
St John's 1555
Jesus 1571

CAMBRIDGE
Christ's 1505
St John's 1509
Magdalene 1542
Trinity 1546
Emmanuel 1584
Sidney Sussex 1589

York
Shrewsbury
Repton 1557
1552
Norwioh
Rugby 1567
Stratford
Cambridge
Harwich
Gloucester
Oxford
Luton
Harrow 1571
London
Highgate 1565
Westminster 1560
Bristol
Sandwich
Guildford
Taunton
Rye
Southampton
Dorchester

0   50
Miles

D

46

DRAKE AND SPAIN 1577–1585

1579

New Albion

St. Augustine

San Domingo

Guinea
Coast

1578

Cartagena

1579

Moluccas

1580

Rio de la Plata

Cape of Good Hope

Straits of Magellan

- ■ Drake leaves Plymouth with 5 ships and 166 men 13 December 1577, and sails around the world
- ▣ Drake siezes Spanish ships and attacks Spaniards on shore
- ✚ Drake takes possession of New Albion (now California) in the name of Queen Elizabeth
- ⊛ Cities captured by Drake in 1585 during the war against Spain

0   3000
Miles

47

LEICESTER'S INTERVENTION IN THE NETHERLANDS 1585

Amsterdam

UNITED NETHERLANDS

Zutphen

❷ New Year's Day 1586 Leicester offered the Stadholdership by the States General.

The Hague

Utrecht

❺ April 1587 Sir Philip Sidney killed in battle of Zutphen. Leicester leaves.

Rhine

Nymegen

❶ December 1585 Leicester lands.

Meuse

❹ December 1586 Leicester relieves siege.

Walcheren I.

Breda

❸ Autumn 1586 Leicester's skirmishes against Parma.

Flushing

Antwerp

SPANISH NETHERLANDS

Bruges

Ypres

Ghent

Maastricht

Brussels

0   25
Miles

Controlled by Spanish under Parma

48

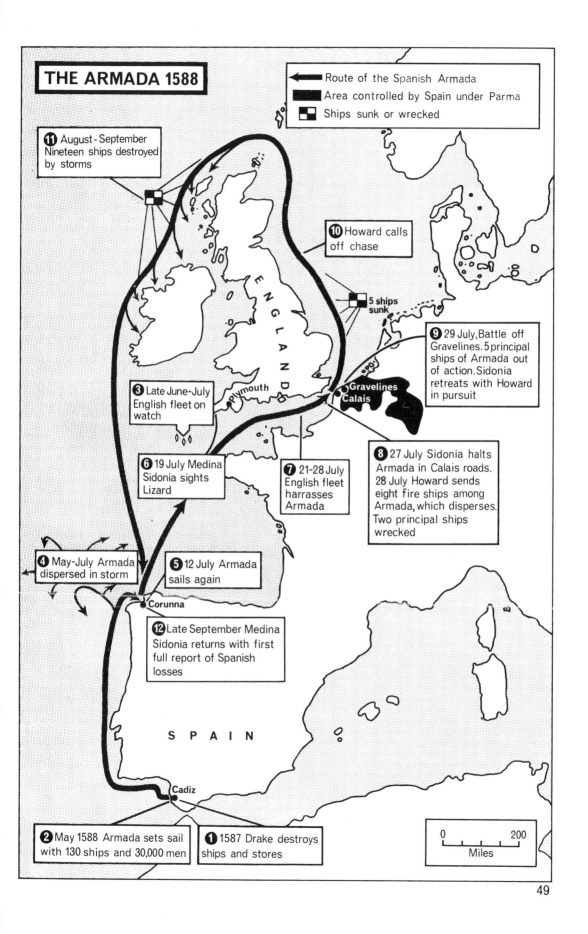

THE ARMADA 1588

Route of the Spanish Armada
Area controlled by Spain under Parma
Ships sunk or wrecked

11 August - September Nineteen ships destroyed by storms

10 Howard calls off chase

5 ships sunk

9 29 July, Battle off Gravelines. 5 principal ships of Armada out of action. Sidonia retreats with Howard in pursuit

3 Late June-July English fleet on watch

ENGLAND

Plymouth

Gravelines
Calais

8 27 July Sidonia halts Armada in Calais roads. 28 July Howard sends eight fire ships among Armada, which disperses. Two principal ships wrecked

6 19 July Medina Sidonia sights Lizard

7 21-28 July English fleet harrasses Armada

4 May-July Armada dispersed in storm

5 12 July Armada sails again

Corunna

12 Late September Medina Sidonia returns with first full report of Spanish losses

S P A I N

Cadiz

2 May 1588 Armada sets sail with 130 ships and 30,000 men

1 1587 Drake destroys ships and stores

0   200
Miles

IRELAND 1603-1625

ULSTER

Londonderry
Belfast
Donegal
Sligo
Carrick
Dundalk
Drogheda
Dublin
Wicklow
Wexford
Limerick
Killarney
Cork
Kinsale

MAYO
GALWAY
CLARE

0   50
Miles

'Planted' before James I

The Plantation of Ulster

Later plantations of James I

51

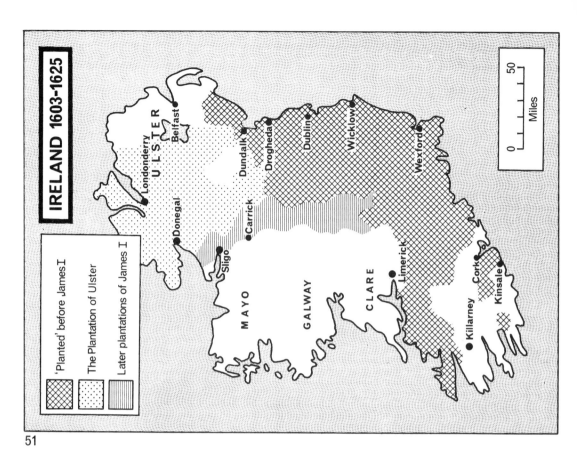

IRELAND 1553-1603

ULSTER

Belfast
Omagh
Enniskillen
Dundalk
Drogheda
Dublin
Wicklow
Wexford
Mullingar
Tuam
Castlebar
Limerick
Tralee
Cork
Kinsale

0   50
Miles

'Planted' (settled) before Mary Tudor

Plantations of Mary Tudor 1553-1558

Plantations of Elizabeth I following revolt of 1569-1573

Plantations of Elizabeth I following revolt of 1601

Other revolts

1601 Spanish landing in support of Irish rebellion

50

THE CARIBBEAN 1562–1717

Slave trading voyages under Sir John Hawkins 1562, 1564, 1567-1569.

English pirate voyage 1589.

English pirate voyage 1596.

English possessions by 1717.

Spanish possessions.

Dutch possessions.

French possessions.

BERMUDA

1609 English settlement.
1684 Transferred to English crown from the Bermuda Company.

1623 English settlement.
1628 Divided with France.
1713 Entirely ceded by Treaty of Utrecht.

ST. KITTS
ANTIGUA
DOMINICA
MARTINIQUE French
CURAÇAO

1625 English
BARBADOS

1617 Raleigh attacks Spaniards but is driven off.

SURINAM

GUIANA

1630 English settlement.
1666 Captured by the Dutch.
1667 Kept by the Dutch, who gave England New Amsterdam (New York) in exchange.

1595 Sir Walter Raleigh searches for Eldorado. On his return writes 'The Discoverie of Guiana.'

TRINIDAD

SPANISH MAIN

1634 Dutch

1669 Morgan sacks Maracaibo and Gibraltar.

Maracaibo
Gibraltar

PUERTO RICO

HISPANIOLA
1697

1646 English settlements.
1703-1717 French and Spanish control.
1717 English.

BAHAMAS

CUBA

JAMAICA

PROVIDENCE ISLAND

Panama
Porto Bello

1671 Morgan attacks Spaniards and sacks Panama.

FLORIDA

1509-1655 Spanish.
1655 Conquered by English.
1670 Formally ceded to England by Spain.

1631-1640 English settlement destroyed by Spaniards.
1666 Recaptured by English buccaneers.

1668 Sir Henry Morgan sacks Porto Bello.

HONDURAS

0   400
Miles

52

THE ORIGINS OF ENGLISH SETTLEMENT IN NEW ENGLAND 1620–1700

London 198

Numbers of emigrants to New England whose county of origin can be traced

THE ORIGINS OF ENGLISH SETTLEMENT IN VIRGINIA 1607–1700

London 179

0   50
Miles

Numbers of emigrants to Virginia whose county of origin can be traced

THE NEW WORLD 1642-1713

CONN. Connecticut
MASS. Massachusetts
N.HAMP. New Hampshire

British possessions 1642
French possessions 1642
Dutch possessions 1642
Swedish possessions 1642
British possessions 1713
French possessions 1713

GASPE

NOVA SCOTIA

A C A D I A

C A N A D A

St. Lawrence

Sault Sainte Marie

Lake Superior

Lake Michigan

Lake Huron

Lake Erie

Lake Ontario

Fort Frontenac

Montreal

Quebec

Detroit

MAINE

Portland

Salem
Boston
Plymouth

Newport
Providence

RHODE ISLAND

N.HAMP.

MASS.

CONN.

Windsor

New Haven

NEW JERSEY

New York

NEW YORK

PENNSYLVANIA

DELAWARE

MARYLAND

St. Mary's

VIRGINIA

Kitty Hawk

NORTH CAROLINA

SOUTH CAROLINA

Ohio

Wabash

Illinois

Mississippi

Wisconsin

Miles

0   200

THE CIVIL WAR 1642–1643

Hull

Adwalton Moor

Belvoir Castle

Worcester

Edge Hill

Oxford

Gloucester

London

Newbury

Pembroke

Taunton

Plymouth

	Districts held by the King 1642
	Districts held by Parliament 1642
	Royalist headquarters
	Parliamentary headquarters
	Charles's first campaign 1642
	Charles's planned campaign for 1643
	Charles's actual campaign in 1643
	Parliamentary garrisons which resisted Charles's sieges 1643
	Charles's gains by December 1643
	Parliamentary gains by 1643

0   50
Miles

THE CIVIL WAR 1644–1646

In May 1646 King Charles surrendered to the Scottish Army at Newark. In February 1647 the Scots sold the King to Parliament for £400,000. He was beheaded on 30 January 1649.

Carlisle

Marston Moor

Hull

Preston
Bolton
Liverpool
Stockport
Sandal Castle
Hulme
Nantwich
Newark
Shrewsbury
Belvoir Castle
Ashby
Lichfield
Naseby
Holmby House
Banbury
Cropredy Bridge
Gloucester
Oxford

Donnington Castle
Bridgewater

Taunton
Lyme Regis
Corfe Castle

Plymouth

The Eastern Association : main recruiting ground for Parliamentary Army 1643

Campaign of Prince Rupert to Marston Moor.

Parliamentary advances to Marston Moor, where the Royalists were defeated 2 July 1644

Area controlled by Parliament in December 1644.

Area gained by Parliament by December 1645.

Districts held by the King in May 1646.

Area gained by Parliament by December 1646.

0   50
Miles

57

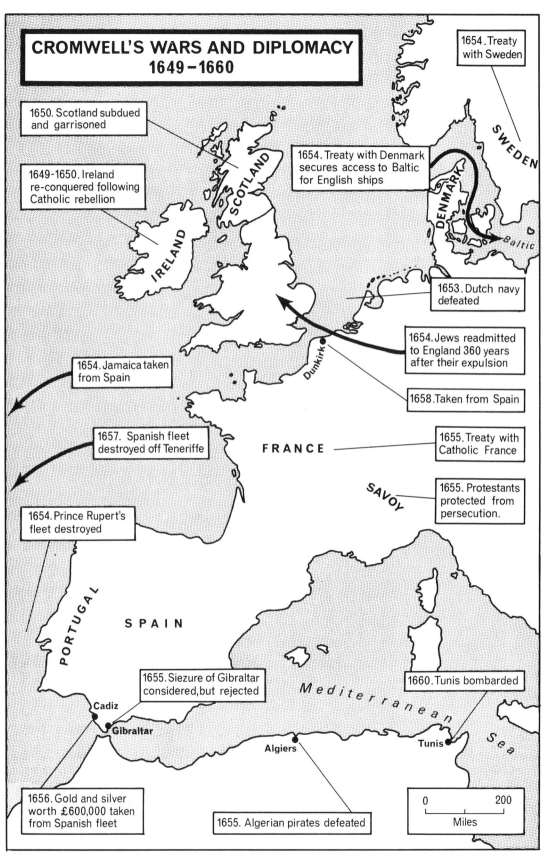

CROMWELL'S WARS AND DIPLOMACY 1649–1660

1654. Treaty with Sweden

1650. Scotland subdued and garrisoned

1654. Treaty with Denmark secures access to Baltic for English ships

1649-1650. Ireland re-conquered following Catholic rebellion

1653. Dutch navy defeated

1654. Jamaica taken from Spain

1654. Jews readmitted to England 360 years after their expulsion

1658. Taken from Spain

1657. Spanish fleet destroyed off Teneriffe

1655. Treaty with Catholic France

1655. Protestants protected from persecution.

1654. Prince Rupert's fleet destroyed

1655. Siezure of Gibraltar considered, but rejected

1660. Tunis bombarded

1656. Gold and silver worth £600,000 taken from Spanish fleet

1655. Algerian pirates defeated

SWEDEN

DENMARK

Baltic

SCOTLAND

IRELAND

Dunkirk

FRANCE

SAVOY

PORTUGAL

SPAIN

Mediterranean Sea

Cadiz

Gibraltar

Algiers

Tunis

0   200
Miles

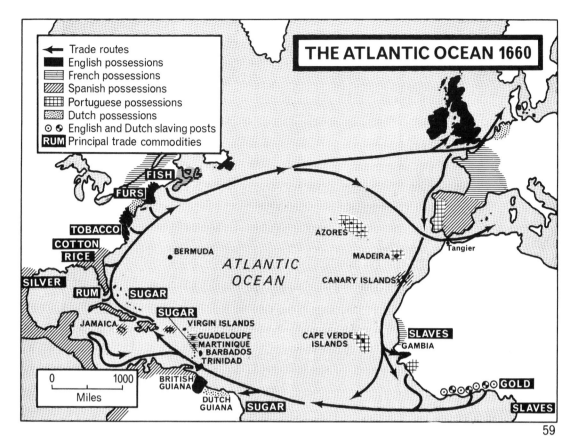

THE ATLANTIC OCEAN 1660

Legend:
- ← Trade routes
- ■ English possessions
- ≡ French possessions
- ⧄ Spanish possessions
- ⊞ Portuguese possessions
- ▒ Dutch possessions
- ⊙ ◉ English and Dutch slaving posts
- RUM Principal trade commodities

FISH
FURS
TOBACCO
COTTON
RICE
SILVER
RUM
SUGAR
SUGAR
JAMAICA
VIRGIN ISLANDS
GUADELOUPE
MARTINIQUE
BARBADOS
TRINIDAD
BRITISH GUIANA
DUTCH GUIANA
SUGAR

BERMUDA
ATLANTIC OCEAN
AZORES
MADEIRA
CANARY ISLANDS
Tangier
CAPE VERDE ISLANDS
SLAVES
GAMBIA
GOLD
SLAVES

0 — 1000
Miles

59

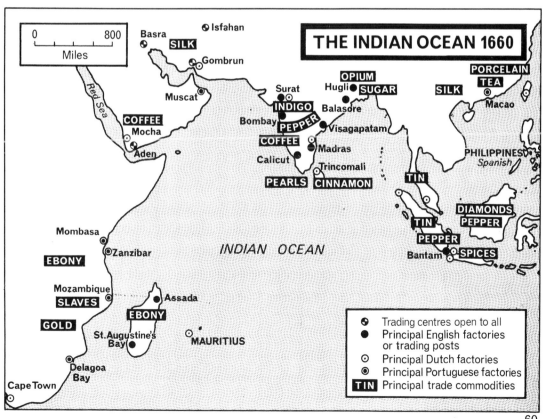

THE INDIAN OCEAN 1660

0 — 800
Miles

Basra
◉ Isfahan
SILK
◉ Gombrun
Muscat
Red Sea
COFFEE
Mocha
Aden

Surat
Hugli
OPIUM
SUGAR
PORCELAIN
TEA
SILK
Macao
INDIGO
Balasore
Bombay
PEPPER
Visagapatam
COFFEE
Madras
Calicut
Trincomali
PEARLS
CINNAMON
PHILIPPINES
Spanish
TIN
DIAMONDS
PEPPER
TIN
PEPPER
Bantam
SPICES

Mombasa
◉ Zanzibar
INDIAN OCEAN
EBONY
Mozambique
SLAVES
GOLD
Assada
EBONY
St. Augustine's Bay
◉ MAURITIUS
Delagoa Bay
Cape Town

Legend:
- ◈ Trading centres open to all
- ● Principal English factories or trading posts
- ⊙ Principal Dutch factories
- ◉ Principal Portuguese factories
- TIN Principal trade commodities

60

THE THREE DUTCH WARS

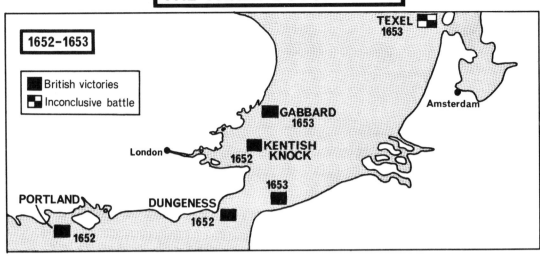

1652-1653

- ■ British victories
- ▣ Inconclusive battle

TEXEL 1653

Amsterdam

GABBARD 1653

London   1652   KENTISH KNOCK

PORTLAND   DUNGENESS

1652   1653   1652

1665-1667

LOWESTOFT ■ 1665

- ← 1665 De Ruyter's expedition up the Medway
- ■ British victories
- ▣ Dutch victories

London

1667 four ships burned in harbour   Chatham   1666   NORTH FORELAND

▣ DOWNS

▣ 1666

▣

0   50
Miles

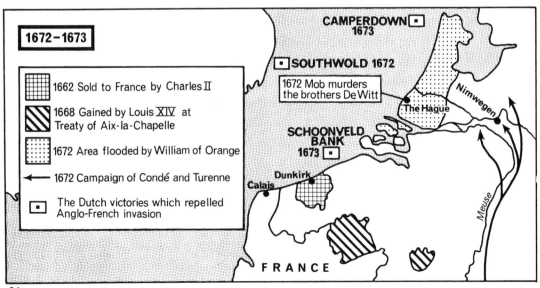

1672-1673

CAMPERDOWN ▣ 1673

▣ SOUTHWOLD 1672

1672 Mob murders the brothers De Witt

The Hague   Nimwegen

- ▦ 1662 Sold to France by Charles II
- ▨ 1668 Gained by Louis XIV at Treaty of Aix-la-Chapelle
- ⠿ 1672 Area flooded by William of Orange
- ← 1672 Campaign of Condé and Turenne
- ▣ The Dutch victories which repelled Anglo-French invasion

SCHOONVELD BANK 1673 ▣

Dunkirk

Calais

Meuse

FRANCE

61

MONMOUTH'S REBELLION 1685

6 3 July Monmouth re-enters Bridgwater

7 5 July Feversham camps at Weston Zoyland

3 Monmouth finds Bristol garrisoned by Feversham for the King

4 Churchill joins Feversham

5 Monmouth beats off a concerted Royalist attack

2 Monmouth welcomed

1 11 June Monmouth lands with 82 supporters

8 6 July Monmouth's army of 3,000 destroyed attempting to break out and attack Royalists by night. 15 July Monmouth beheaded

London
Thames
Bristol
Bath
Norton St.Philip
Bridgwater
Taunton
Sedgemoor
Lyme Regis

⟵ Route of Monmouth's campaign 1685
⟸ Movement of Royalist army 1685

0   25
Miles

THE GLORIOUS REVOLUTION 1688

2 English army converges on Salisbury and Churchill is given command of the troops

5 25 Nov. Churchill deserts James with 400 cavalry and goes over to William

3 Cornbury deserts to William with 200 cavalry

6 James returns to Whitehall. The Queen and James' heir escape to France via Gravesend followed by James on 11 Dec. after throwing the Great Seal into the Thames.

4 19 Nov. James arrives from Windsor

1 5 Nov. William of Orange lands with 15,000 men

Thames
Windsor
London
Hungerford
Wilton
Salisbury
Southampton
Honiton
Crewkerne
Exeter
Axminster
Brixham
Tor Bay

⟸ Movement of the English army 1688
⟵ Route of William's campaign 1688

0   25
Miles

IRELAND 1689-1691

Belfast

Londonderry

Enniskillen

Newtown Butler

4 Protestants win control of Ulster July 1689

Boyne

Dublin

5 July 1690. Battle of the Boyne William III defeats James II

3 Sieges of Londonderry and Enniskillen, relieved by William III's forces

2 Irish Catholics attack Ulster

6 July 1691 Final defeat of Irish-French forces

Aughrim

Galway

Limerick

1 March 1689. James II and French force land

7 1691 14,000 Irish soldiers go into exile to France, and join the French Army

The greater part of William's forces were Dutch, Danes and Huguenots

0 — 50
Miles

65

IRELAND 1649-1651

→ Cromwell's reconquests 1649, following Catholic rebellion of 1641

■ Stormed by Cromwell: garrisons and priests murdered

▤ Lands given by Cromwell to the veterans of his Parliamentary Army

▦ Reservations for the transplanted Irish (but land four miles inland from all shores was reserved for the English)

Drogheda

Dublin

Wexford

Ross

Kilkenny

Carrick

Clonmel

Sligo

Castlebar

Tuam

Limerick

1651. Besieged by Ireton

Killarney

Cromwell established free trade between Ireland and England. Ireland gained equal access to foreign and colonial markets; and received thirty seats in the London Parliament. The large landowners were now Protestants, the small farmers and peasants Catholics

0 — 50
Miles

64

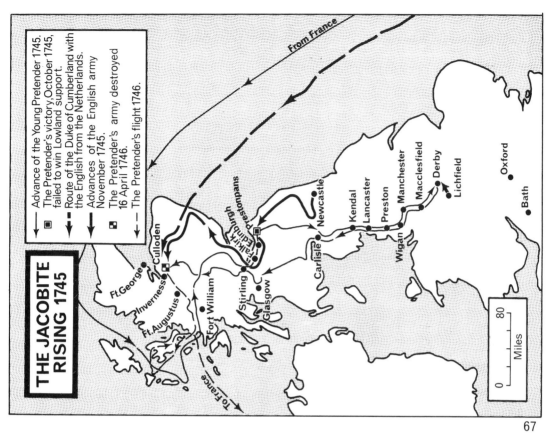

THE JACOBITE RISING 1745

Legend:
→ Advance of the Young Pretender 1745.
■ The Pretender's victory, October 1745, failed to win Lowland support.
⇢ Route of the Duke of Cumberland with the English from the Netherlands.
→ Advances of the English army November 1745.
■ The Pretender's army destroyed 16 April 1746.
- - - The Pretender's flight 1746.

From France

Ft.George
Culloden
Inverness
Ft.Augustus
Fort William
Stirling
Glasgow
Edinburgh
Falkirk
Prestonpans
Newcastle
Carlisle
Kendal
Lancaster
Preston
Wigan
Manchester
Macclesfield
Derby
Lichfield
Oxford
Bath
To France

0   80
Miles

THE JACOBITE RISING 1715

Legend:
■ Area from which the Jacobite risings gained support.
⇨ Advance of Mar in support of the Old Pretender
→ Route of the Border Country rising
■ Jacobite defeats

Peterhead
Inverness
Fort Ruthven
Perth
Sheriffmuir
Edinburgh
Melrose
Carlisle
Kendal
Lancaster
Preston
Oxford
Marlborough
Bath
Wells

0   80
Miles

THE WAR OF THE SPANISH SUCCESSION 1702-1713

0   50

Miles

UNITED PROVINCES (HOLLAND)

S P A N I S H

Oudenarde 1708

Maastricht

Ramillies 1706

1702

Liège

Malplaquet 1709

NETHERLANDS

ELECTORATE OF COLOGNE

Meuse

Rhine

TO BRANDENBURG

Cologne

Bonn

➡️ Marlborough's march to the Danube

■ Fortresses held by the French

▣ Fortresses held by the Allies

⇢ Movements of Eugene of Saxony after the meeting of the Allied forces

→ Movements of the French and Bavarian armies under Tallard

▲▲▲▲ The Lines of Stolhofen

◪ Other British victories

Coblenz

Limburg 1703

Moselle

Trarbach

Trier

Mainz

Landau

Philippsburg

Frankfurt

SAXONY (Part of)

From any position on the Rhine Marlborough's army can return to Flanders by river faster than Tallard's can march.

Meuse

F R A N C E

Rhine

Strasbourg

Kehl

13 Aug.1704. Victory at Blenheim for England and Austria over France and Bavaria.

Old Breisach

Freiburg

Villingen

Ulm

Ingolstadt

Danube

2 July. Fortresses of Schellenburg & Donauwörth taken by the Allies.

B A V A R I A

England, Holland, Portugal, Savoy, Brandenburg, Saxony and Austria allied against France, Spain, Bavaria and the Electorate of Cologne.

H A B S B U R G AUSTRIA

THE PEACE OF UTRECHT 1713

1707 Union between Scotland and England

HUDSON BAY

St Lawrence

NEWFOUNDLAND

NOVA SCOTIA

FLORIDA

CUBA

MEXICO

Britain obtains right to load vessels of 500 tons capacity with tropical produce

11 April 1713 France makes peace with Britain, Holland, Savoy and Portugal.
13 June 1713 Spain makes peace with Britain.
Not until 26 June 1714 is peace concluded between Spain and Holland.

Stettin

Lingen
Gelden
SPANISH NETHERLANDS

GREAT BRITAIN

FRANCE

MILAN
SAVOY

KINGDOM OF NAPLES

SICILY

SARDINIA

Minorca

SPAIN

Gibraltar

	To be ruled by the House of Bourbon. But the kingdoms of France and Spain not to be united
	Annexed by the House of Habsburg
	Annexed by Savoy
	Annexed by Britain
	Transferred to the Elector of Brandenburg.
◑	Fortresses given to the control of the Dutch
■	British trading rights gained in the Atlantic and Caribbean
▲	

Britain obtains right to transport 4,800 African slaves each year to Spanish America

E

69

THE BRITISH CONQUEST OF CANADA 1758-1760

⑥ 17 September 1759, French capitulate. Death of Wolfe

④ 1758-1759, Britain's Red Indian allies harass French and drive them from the Lakes

⑦ 1760, triple British advance on Montreal where the French finally surrender

② 26 July 1758, French surrender

⑤ June- September 1759, Wolfe's expedition

① 8 July 1758, French hold fort against British assault. 2000 out of 15,000 British troops killed

③ 24 November 1758, blown up by French as they retreated

French possessions, 1756

Miles

0   300

St. John

Beauséjour

Port Royal

Ticonderoga

Boston

New York

THE THIRTEEN COLONIES

Quebec

Heights of Abraham

Montreal

Fort Frontenac

Lake Ontario

Lake Erie

Fort Duquesne

Fort Miamis

Fort St. Joseph

Lake Huron

Lake Michigan

Lake Superior

Fort Nipigon

Fort St. Pierre

Fort St. Esprit

Fort Crèveceour

Fort Vincennes

THE BRITISH EMPIRE 1763

10 February 1763 The Treaty of Paris ended the Seven Years' War. France ceded Canada and the Mississippi Valley to Britain.

BENGAL
MASULIPATAM
MADRAS
FORT YORK
BOMBAY

MINORCA
GIBRALTAR
ST. LOUIS
FORT JAMES
CAPE COAST CASTLE
ST. HELENA

GREAT BRITAIN
IRELAND
NEWFOUNDLAND

THE THIRTEEN COLONIES
BERMUDAS
FLORIDA
BAHAMAS
JAMAICA
BARBADOS
CANADA
Mississippi
HUDSON BAY COMPANY
HONDURAS
MOSQUITO COAST

The British Empire 1763

71

THE EUROPEAN POWERS IN INDIA 1510-1775

1757 Bengalis defeated.

1764 rulers of Oudh and Murshidabad defeated.

1770 famine kills a third of the natives of Bengal.

SIKHS

RAJPUTS

OUDH

Benares

Buxar 1764

MURSHIDABAD

BENGAL

Plassey 1757

Chandernagore French 1673

Calcutta British 1690

1773-1912 Capital of British India.

Fredriksnagar Danish 1616-1845

DIU IS. Portuguese 1515

Daman Portuguese 1558

Bassein Portuguese 1534-1739

Bombay Portuguese 1534: British 1661

MAHRATTAS

NORTHERN CIRCARS

French 1752 British 1766

Yanaon French 1750

GOA Portuguese 1510-1961

Pulicat Dutch 1609-1825

Mangalore Portuguese 1596-1673

MADRAS British 1644

1760 French defeated.

Wandiwash

Mahé French 1726

Cannanore Dutch 1656-1791

Pondicherry French 1683

Capital of French India.

Tranquebar Danish 1620-1845

MALABAR COAST

Karikal French 1739

1706 first Protestant (Lutheran) missionary settlement in India.

Negapatam Dutch 1660-1781

COROMANDEL COAST

Cochin Dutch 1663-1775

Jaffna Portuguese 1617-1658 Dutch 1658-1795

Trincomali Dutch 1639-1795

MALDIVE IS. Dutch 1645-1796

CEYLON

Colombo Portuguese 1517-1656 Dutch 1656-1796

0   200

Miles

British victories

British Territory 1775

THE REVOLT OF THE AMERICAN COLONIES 1774-1783

⇨ British campaigns, assisted after 1775 by 29,000 mercenaries hired in Germany.

➤ Rebel campaigns. George Washington made Commander-in-Chief 1775.

⑤ Summer 1775 taken by rebels

② May 1775 seized by rebels

① 19 April 1775 first outbreak of of rebellion dispersed by the British who destroy rebel military stores

④ Besieged by rebels, April 1775 to March 1776, when British withdrew

⑥ 17 October 1777 British force under Burgoyne surrenders

③ 17 June 1775 rebels defeated

⑪ 19 October 1781 British surrender ensures final rebel victory

⑦ 1778 George Rogers Clark defeats British along the Ohio River

⑩ 1781 French naval blockade prevents British Fleet from going to the aid of Cornwallis

⑧ 1778-1780 captured and controlled by British

⑨ 1781 British under Cornwallis fail to conquer the Carolinas and Virginia

Many loyal colonists settled in the Bermudas after the defeat of the British

4 July 1776 Declaration of Independence by rebels
1778 Rebels ally with France
1783 Peace signed at Paris. Britain recognises the independence of the Thirteen Colonies

Lake Superior
Lake Huron
Lake Michigan
Lake Ontario
Lake Erie
St. Lawrence
Montreal
Ticonderoga
Saratoga
Lexington
Bunker Hill
Boston
New York
PENNSYLVANIA
VIRGINIA
Yorktown
Ohio
NORTH CAROLINA
Wilmington
SOUTH CAROLINA
Mississippi

0   200
Miles

73

AGRICULTURE 1700–1800

Stirling

1758. First threshing machine.
1786. Improved threshing machine

Carlisle

Newcastle

Durham
Durham Shorthorns

York

Leeds

Hull

Sheffield

Manchester

Liverpool

Coke's estates a showpiece of improved farming

Lord Townshend introduces the turnip and four fold rotation of crops.

Lynn Holkham

Bakewell reforms breeding of sheep & cattle.

Elkington introduces deep trench drains.

Worcester

Herefords

Jethro Tull introduces the seed drill.

Gloucester

Chelmsford

Oxford

1793. Board of Agriculture set up.

Bristol

Windsor

London

Salisbury

Southdowns

Winchester

George III's model farm

Enclosures in the eighteenth century

▅ intense
▦ widespread ⎫ enclosure
⎯ some ⎭
░ Young's tours of England from 1763
▒ New breeds of sheep and cattle

0   50
Miles

INDUSTRY 1715–1815

Legend:
- Coalfields
- Coalbrookdale iron works, where Abraham Darby first successfully used coke for smelting, 1709, and where Newcomen's steam-powered pump was first used
- Area of Sheffield steel industry improved by Huntsman's refining techniques from 1760
- Growing towns
- New coal-fired iron works
- Burslem, Wedgwood's factory founded 1759
- Major dock developments
- Business kings of Lancashire and Yorkshire

POPULATION OF LARGEST TOWNS 1801

London	864,000
Manchester	84,000
Edinburgh	82,500
Glasgow	77,300
Liverpool	77,000
Birmingham	73,000
Bristol	68,000
Leeds	53,000

1775. Watt's first efficient steam engine

Glasgow
Edinburgh
Newcastle

1779 Crompton's mule developed

1733. John Kay's first flying shuttle

1764. Hargreaves invents Spinning Jenny

Benjamin Gott
Leeds
Hull
Bradford
Preston
Halifax
Bolton   Bury
Manchester
Robert Peel
Liverpool
Stockport   Sheffield
Samuel Oldknow

1785. Cartwright builds power loom

Chester
Broseley   Derby   Nottingham
Stoke
1770-1808 Wilkinson's iron-works
Stafford
Leicester

1769 Arkwright's spinning machine

1773-1779. First cast-iron bridge built

Shrewsbury
Coalbrookdale
Bridgnorth   Birmingham
Bewdley   Coventry

1748. Paul invents wool carding

LONDON DOCKS
East India
West India
London
Commercial
Surrey

Merthyr
Swansea   Neath

Bristol
Bath

1754. Cort's first iron rolling machine

London

1779. First steam powered mills

Southampton

China Clay

0   50
Miles

TRANSPORT 1760–1830

41 hours to London by Mail Coach

The first British census was taken in 1801:
England 8,331,434
Scotland 1,599,068
Wales 541,546
Total 10,472,048

Mail Packet to Belfast

Mail Packet to Dublin

28 Hours to London by Mail Coach

32 Hours to London by Mail Coach

1830 Telford drains part of the Fens

21 Hours to London by Mail Coach

1770's Brindley builds over 365 miles of canals

16 Hours to London by Mail Coach

Mail Packet to Waterford

Mail Packet to Amsterdam

Mail Packet to Calais

1828 Telford completes St. Katherine's Docks

Mail Packet to the Channel Islands

Mail Packet to New York

Places: Stirling, Glasgow, Port Patrick, Carlisle, Newcastle, Sunderland, Whitehaven, Appleby, Hull, Liverpool, Manchester, Grimsby, Holyhead, Birmingham, Lynn, Great Yarmouth, Bury St. Edmunds, Harwich, Milford Haven, Oxford, London, Bristol, Wey, Guildford, Dover, Weymouth, Plymouth, Falmouth, Arun

Rivers/Canals: Bridgewater, Trent & Mersey, Trent, Soar, Wreak, Nene, Grand Junction, Lugg, Severn, Avon, Oxford, Wye, Thames, Kennet and Avon

——	Major canals built 1760–1820
	Major road improvements by Telford 1804–1828
	General Wade's road works
	Metcalf's road works
	Other important road improvements
⊕	Ports being developed

0   50
Miles

BRITISH EXPANSION IN INDIA 1775–1858

British India 1775.
Expansion by 1806.
Expansion by 1836.
Expansion by 1856.

Main centres of the Indian Mutiny of 1857

Peshawar

PUNJAB

ROHILKHAND — KUMAON

Delhi — Lucknow

Bikaner

Ajmer — Gwalior

DOAB — OUDH

RAJPUTANA

SIND

Udaipur

BUNDELKHAND

Indore

Baroda

GUJARAT

NAGPUR

BERAR

NIZAM'S DOMINIONS

Hyderabad

Bombay

ASSAM

BIHAR

BENGAL

Dacca

Dum Dum

Calcutta

ARAKAN

Cuttack

NORTHERN CIRCARS

PEGU

ANDAMAN ISLANDS
1858 British convict settlement

TENASSERIM

MYSORE
MALABAR
CARNATIC
Madras

1834 British rule.
1881 Native rajah restored.

COCHIN
TRAVANCORE

CEYLON
1815 British sovereignty.

MALDIVE ISLANDS
1796 British.

0   400
Miles

THE WAR AGAINST FRANCE 1793–1802

Principal campaigns on land 1793 – 1801

First Coalition against France 1793

Second Coalition against France 1798

1793 France declares war on Britain.
1794 France invades Holland.
1798 France annexes left bank of the Rhine and declares war on Naples.
1801 France makes peace with Austria, Naples and Ottoman Empire.
1802 Peace of Amiens between Britain and France.

7 1 August 1798, Nelson destroys the French Fleet.

Nile

EGYPT

OTTOMAN EMPIRE

RUSSIA

AUSTRIA

PRUSSIA

Belgrade

Cracow

9 September 1800, captured by British.

MALTA

KINGDOM OF NAPLES

SICILY

Naples

Rome

SARDINIA

MINORCA

8 November 1798, captured by British.

0   200
Miles

HOLLAND

Rhine

5 11 October 1797, Duncan defeats Dutch.

Camperdown

Amiens

Paris

FRANCE

The Nore

Spithead

GREAT BRITAIN

4 15 April – 16 June 1797, naval mutinies.

1 1 June 1794 Howe defeats French.

2 June – October 1795 risings in Brittany aided by Britain.

6 1798 French invasion attempt fails.

SPAIN

PORTUGAL

Cape St. Vincent

3 14 February 1797, Jarvis and Nelson defeat Spaniards.

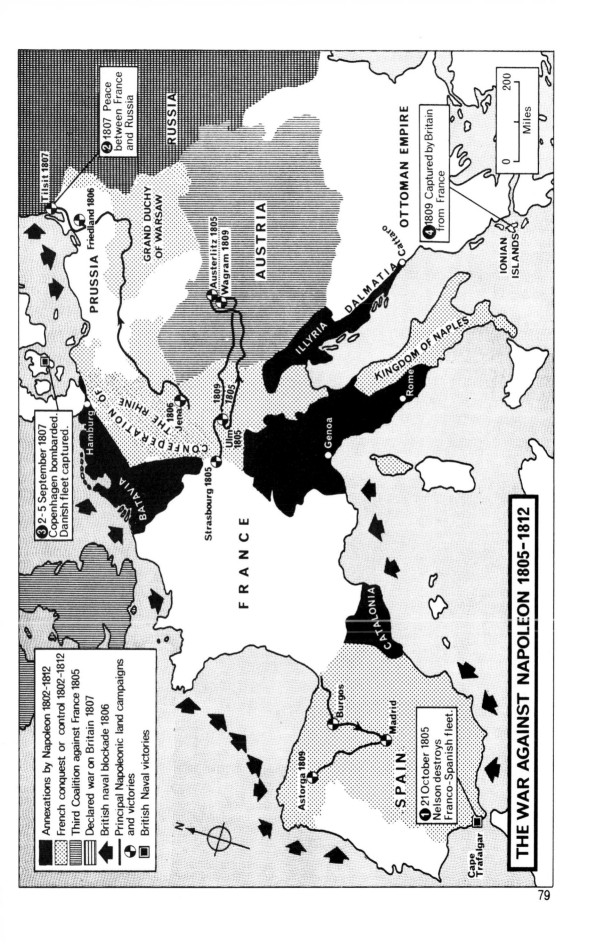

THE WAR AGAINST NAPOLEON 1805–1812

Legend:
- Annexations by Napoleon 1802–1812
- French conquest or control 1802–1812
- Third Coalition against France 1805
- Declared war on Britain 1807
- British naval blockade 1806
- Principal Napoleonic land campaigns and victories
- British Naval victories

❶ 21 October 1805 Nelson destroys Franco-Spanish fleet.

❷ 1807 Peace between France and Russia

❸ 2–5 September 1807 Copenhagen bombarded. Danish fleet captured.

❹ 1809 Captured by Britain from France

RUSSIA

PRUSSIA

Tilsit 1807

Friedland 1806

GRAND DUCHY OF WARSAW

AUSTRIA

Austerlitz 1805
Wagram 1809

ILLYRIA

DALMATIA

Cattaro

OTTOMAN EMPIRE

IONIAN ISLANDS

KINGDOM OF NAPLES

Rome

Genoa

CONFEDERATION OF THE RHINE

Hamburg

Jena 1806

Ulm 1805

1809

1805

BATAVIA

Strasbourg 1805

FRANCE

CATALONIA

Burgos

Madrid

Astorga 1809

SPAIN

Cape Trafalgar

0   200
Miles

79

THE PENINSULAR WAR 1808-1814

F R A N C E

Toulouse

MINORCA

⑤ 10 April 1814
Wellington defeats
the French

④ 7 October 1813
Wellington crosses
into France.

BRITISH NAVAL CONTROL

② 1809 French attack
into Andalusia

British campaigns.
French control 1809.
French control 1811.
Spanish guerilla activity 1808-1813.

Burgos

1813-1814

1811

Madrid

1812

Valladolid

1812

1812

Talavera

1813

Ciudad Rodrigo

1809

A N D A L U S I A

Gibraltar

Cadiz

BRITISH NAVAL CONTROL

Coruña

1808

1809

Almeida

1811

P O R T U G A L

Badajoz

③ Winter 1810 French
forced to retire through
starvation.

Sierra Busaco

1811

Torres Vedras

Lisbon

1808-1812 British troops

① 1808 Spaniards
force French army
to surrender.

0   80

Miles

THE DEFEAT OF NAPOLEON 1812–1815

① May 1812 Napoleon invades Russia.

③ September–October 1812 Napoleon in Moscow. Then retreats.

④ November 1813 Dutch rising against the French.

⑧ 18 June 1815 Napoleon defeated. Abdicates. Exiled to St. Helena, a British island in the Southern Atlantic.

⑥ March 1814 Entered by the Allies. Napoleon abdicates and is exiled to Elba.

⑤ Rising of inhabitants in favour of Bourbons.

② August 1812 Wellington enters Madrid.

⑦ March 1815 Napoleon escapes and lands in France.

Napoleon's Empire 1812.

Under French control or influence 1812.

Napoleon's advance to Moscow.

Napoleon's retreat from Moscow.

Countries allied against Napoleon 1813–1814.

French victories.

Allied victories.

Napoleon's return from exile in Elba.

⊕ ◒

SWEDEN

GREAT BRITAIN

DENMARK

RUSSIA

Moscow

Borodino

Beresina

PRUSSIA

GRAND DUCHY OF WARSAW

Berlin

Leipzig

Dresden

AUSTRIA

CONFEDERATION OF THE RHINE

SWISS CONFEDERATION

KINGDOM OF ITALY

KINGDOM OF NAPLES

Cattaro

ELBA

Fréjus

Waterloo

Brussels

Paris

Bordeaux

Vitoria

Madrid

SPAIN

PORTUGAL

0   300

Miles

THE WAR AGAINST THE UNITED STATES 1812-1815

CANADA

Moose Island
7 November 1813 Captured by British

10 Mar. 1814 200 British repulse 4000 Americans

La Colle Mill

Montreal
Plattsburg
Sacket's Harbour
Kingston
Oswego

Boston

12 Aug. 1814 British troops defeat U.S. troops at Plattsburg. Sept.1814 U.S. fleet defeats British fleet on Lake Champlain

11 May 1814 British raid.

13 British burn the Capitol and White House ; raid Alexandria and Baltimore

5 U.S. proposal to march into Canada from here does not materialise

4 April 1813 Successful U.S. attack

York
Newark
Buffalo

BRITISH NAVAL BLOCKADE

Baltimore
Washington
Alexandria

9 Dec. 1813 Burnt by British as reprisal

Fort Mackinac

2 17 July 1812 Captured by British

Ohio

8 November 1813 U.S. forces burn Newark

6 October 1813 U.S. victory

3 16 August 1812 U.S. forces surrender

1 June 1812 U.S. forces advance towards Canada

In 1811 British ships seized US sailors and forced them to join the Royal Navy. The British in Canada supported Indian tribes raiding south of the Great Lakes. Britain also blockaded US ports to prevent American trade with Napoleon. In June 1812 the US declared war on Britain.

Mississippi

14 British fail to capture New Orleans after initial successes. They withdraw 27 January 1815. Neither side was aware that the war had officially ended before the battle of New Orleans.

Mobile
Pensacola

New Orleans
Fort St. Philip

0   200
Miles

THE BRITISH EMPIRE 1820

NEW SOUTH WALES

PENANG
MALACCA
SINGAPORE

INDIA
BENGAL
MADRAS
FORT YORK

BOMBAY
CEYLON
MALDIVES

LACCADIVES
CHAGOS

SEYCHELLES

MAURITIUS

HELIGOLAND

IONIAN ISLANDS

MALTA

CAPE COLONY

GAMBIA
SIERRA LEONE
NIGER
GOLD COAST
ASCENSION

ST. HELENA

BRITISH ISLES

GIBRALTAR

NEWFOUNDLAND

LABRADOR

BERMUDA

BAHAMAS

ST. LUCIA
TOBAGO
TRINIDAD
BARBADOS

JAMAICA

BRITISH GUIANA

C A N A D A

BRITISH HONDURAS

The British Empire 1820

British gains as a result
of the Napoleonic wars

Territory claimed by
the United States

83

PARLIAMENTARY REPRESENTATION BEFORE 1832

The pattern of population density 1830

Areas of greatest population increase since 1760 mainly as a result of the industrial revolution, and the movement of people from the land to the towns

Sparsely populated

○ Large towns with no Members of Parliament

● Rotten boroughs

Sunderland

Bradford Leeds
Blackburn Halifax
Bolton Oldham
Manchester Stockport Sheffield
Macclesfield

Stoke

Wolverhampton Birmingham

Cheltenham

Stroud

Greenwich

Old Sarum Portsmouth Brighton

Devonport

0 ____ 50
Miles

All Counties returned two Members of Parliament regardless of their population

PARLIAMENTARY REFORM 1832

NORTHUMBERLAND

Tynemouth
Gateshead South Shields
Sunderland

DURHAM

CUMBERLAND

Whitehaven

Kendal   Whitby

YORKSHIRE

LANCASHIRE
Blackburn
Bolton Leeds
Bury Oldham Bradford
Salford Halifax Wakefield
Stockport Huddersfield
Warrington Ashton
Manchester Sheffield
Macclesfield

CHESHIRE

LINCOLN

Stoke DERBY

NOTTINGHAM

SHROPSHIRE STAFFORD

NORFOLK

Walsall LEICESTER

Wolverhampton
Dudley Birmingham NORTHAMPTON

SUFFOLK

Kidderminster WARWICK CAMBRIDGE

HEREFORD WORCS HERTFORD ESSEX

Cheltenham OXFORD BUCKINGHAM

Stroud Marylebone
GLOUCESTER Tower Hamlets
Merthyr BERKSHIRE Finsbury Greenwich
Tydfil Lambeth Chatham
Frome WILTSHIRE SURREY KENT
HAMPSHIRE
SUSSEX Brighton
SOMERSET

DORSET ISLE OF
DEVON WIGHT

Devonport
CORNWALL

●	Towns enfranchised with two Members of Parliament
⊙	Towns enfranchised with one Member of Parliament
(horizontal lines)	Counties gaining two extra Members of Parliament
(dark stipple)	Counties gaining one extra Member of Parliament

IRELAND 1880–1882

Belfast

Londonderry

Dublin

Kilmainham Gaol

Cork

Ballin

Ennis

Killarney

❸ October 1880, fifty Ulstermen and 900 soldiers march to harvest crops on Lord Erne's land (managed by Captain Boycott).

❷ Lord Erne's lands, attacked by peasantry, September 1880.

❻ 6 May 1882. Lord Cavendish and Thomas Burke murdered in Phœnix Park.

❺ 13 October 1881. Parnell imprisoned under new Coercion Act, passed March 1881. 2 May 1882, Parnell released.

❹ 1880. Seamen refuse to ship cattle bound for England.

❶ 19 September 1880 : Parnell preaches doctrine of boycotting.

○ Overpopulation
◉ Centres of industrial growth 1800-1900

0   50
Miles

IRELAND 1789–1861

Tone

Belfast

Dungannon

Castlebar

Dublin

Galway

Ballinasloe

Vinegar Hill

Cork

F A M I N E 1846

2,000,000 died of starvation 1,800,000 fled to USA 1846-1861

1801. Union of Great Britain and Ireland. British and Irish Parliaments combine. All Irish legislation made in London until 1922.

1829. Parliament passes Catholic Emancipation Act.

1798. The attempted invasion by France in support of United Irishmen arrived too late.

▥ Area with over 50% protestant population. Home of Orange Society formed to resist Catholic Union Irishmen
◓ Ports for emigration to USA and Britain
✪ Battles of the 1798 rising of the United Irishmen

0   50
Miles

LABOUR MOVEMENTS 1819–1910

- ◓ Early labour agitation 1819-1843
- ◎ Centres of Chartism 1836-1854
- ◉ Headquarters of Chartism 1839
- ⊜ Chartist Agricultural Settlements
- ▨ Agitation for Factory Act reform
- ☰ The Miners' Strike 1893
- ○ First working men returned to Parliament before 1906
- ● Labour Party Members elected to Parliament 1906

◎ Glasgow

○ New Lanark

1820's Robert Owen's model mills

1871. Successful strike of engineers for nine hour day

Morpeth 1874 ○

Newcastle ◎

Middlesbrough ○ 1892

1893. Miners' strike. 2 miners killed when troops fire on rioters.

Trade Union members
1888	750,000
1901	2,025,000
1910	2,565,000

Rochdale

Halifax

◎ Leeds

Manchester ◎ Cooperative Movement 1843

Peterloo Massacre 1819

Sheffield

Derby

1901

Nottingham

Stafford 1874

Norwich

Leicester

1893. Miners' strike. Attempt to close South Wales pits defeated in pitched battle with hauliers.

Birmingham

1889. First strikes of unskilled labour -match girls and dockers for 6d. an hour. Both succeed.

Ipswich ◎

Merthyr Tydfil 1901

Ebbw Vale ○

Carterton

Watford

Riots 1839

London

Newport

Bath

Speenhamland

Rochester

Chatham

◎ Trowbridge

Martyrs 1834 Tolpuddle

LEGISLATIVE ADVANCES

1819. Young workers restricted to a 12 hour working day
1824. Working men allowed to combine
1842. Female labour underground forbidden
1871. Trade Unions legalized
1874. Factory Act restricts working week to 56½ hours
1882. Married Women's Property Act enables women to buy, own, and sell property and to keep all wages and earnings
1906-1911. Lloyd George launches National Insurance Scheme, and establishes Port of London Authority. Churchill abolishes sweated labour, forbids underground employment of boys under fourteen, introduces minimum wage law, improves shop conditions, establishes Labour Exchanges to reduce unemployment, and makes prison conditions more humane

0 _____ 50
Miles

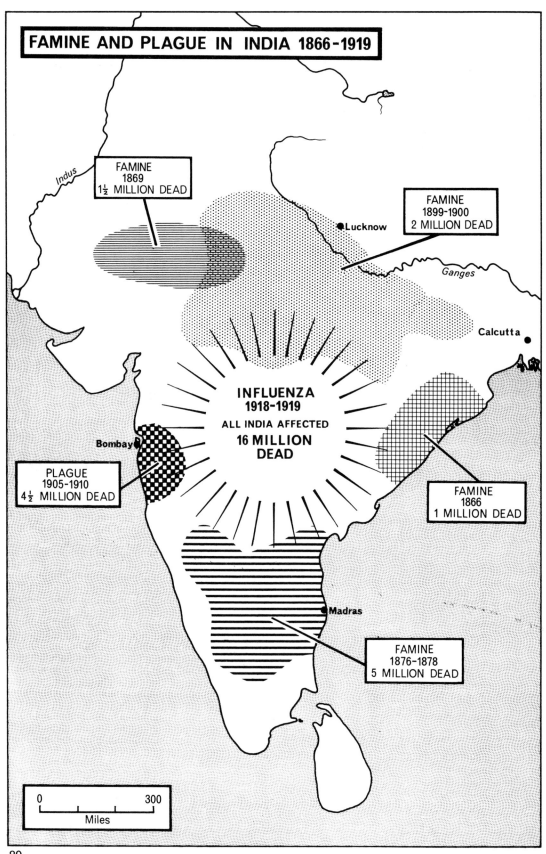

FAMINE AND PLAGUE IN INDIA 1866-1919

FAMINE
1869
1½ MILLION DEAD

FAMINE
1899-1900
2 MILLION DEAD

Indus

Lucknow

Ganges

Calcutta

INFLUENZA
1918-1919
ALL INDIA AFFECTED
16 MILLION
DEAD

Bombay

PLAGUE
1905-1910
4½ MILLION DEAD

FAMINE
1866
1 MILLION DEAD

Madras

FAMINE
1876-1878
5 MILLION DEAD

0   300
Miles

RAILWAYS 1825–1914

The Stockton and Darlington Railway, opened in 1825.

The Liverpool and Manchester Railway, opened in 1830.

Glasgow
Edinburgh
Ayr
Carlisle
Newcastle
Sunderland
Lancaster
York
Hull
Holyhead
Crewe
Lincoln
Ruabon
Birmingham
Rugby
Norwich
Cambridge
Gloucester
Colchester
Merthyr
Oxford
London
Cardiff
Bristol
Salisbury
Dover
Brighton
Exeter

	Railways by 1836: 1,000 miles built
	Railways by 1852: 7,000 miles built
	Railways by 1914: 23,000 miles built

0   50
Miles

BRITAIN IN THE FAR EAST 1788-1914

Penal colonies for convicts transported from Britain 1788-1840

British possessions 1914

PHOENIX ISLANDS 1889

TONGA

1900 Britain conducts foreign affairs and guarantees local autonomy

ELLICE ISLANDS 1892

FIJI 1874

NEW ZEALAND

GILBERT ISLANDS 1892

SOLOMON ISLANDS 1893

NORFOLK ISLAND 1853

LORD HOWE ISLAND 1788

N

PAPUA 1884

QUEENSLAND

A U S T R A L I A

NEW SOUTH WALES

Botany Bay 1788

TASMANIA 1803

NORTHERN TERRITORY

SOUTH AUSTRALIA

VICTORIA

Port Philip 1835

WESTERN AUSTRALIA

HONG KONG 1842

NTH. BORNEO 1888

SARAWAK 1888

LABUAN 1846

SINGAPORE 1819

COCOS ISLANDS 1857

1901 Australia becomes a Commonwealth in British Empire 1907 New Zealand becomes a self-governing Dominion

MALAYA 1874-96

BURMA 1886

ANDAMAN ISLANDS 1858

NICOBAR ISLANDS 1869

0   1000

Miles

BRITAIN AND CHINA 1840-1945

MANCHURIA

Russian occupation1900
Japanese occupation1905

KOREA

Japanese 1910

JAPAN

Japanese 1895

WEI HAI WEI 1898-1922

SHANGHAI 1842

FORMOSA

Japanese 1895

Wuhu 1876

Ningpo 1842

Amoy 1842

Tungchow1858

Peking

1900. Boxer rebellion against all Europeans

Canton1842

KOWLOON 1891

HONG KONG 1842

KIUNGCHOW 1858

1840-1842 First China War: Hong Kong ceded to Britain.
1857-1858 Second China War; Anglo-French control of Chinese Customs Administration extended.
1900 Britain joined other powers to suppress Boxer rebellion.

Chungking1896

Yangtse

FRENCH INDO-CHINA

SIAM

S I N K I A N G

1919-1941 Russian influence

T I B E T

N E P A L

BHUTAN 1910

SIKKIM 1890

ASSAM 1826

BURMA 1886

1940-1945. British military aid sent to help China against Japan

KASHMIR 1846

DELHI 1815

I N D I A

0   500

Miles

● British territory in China

British territory outside China

Treaty Ports open to all European trade without restriction

Important British-sponsored explorations 1890-1910

92

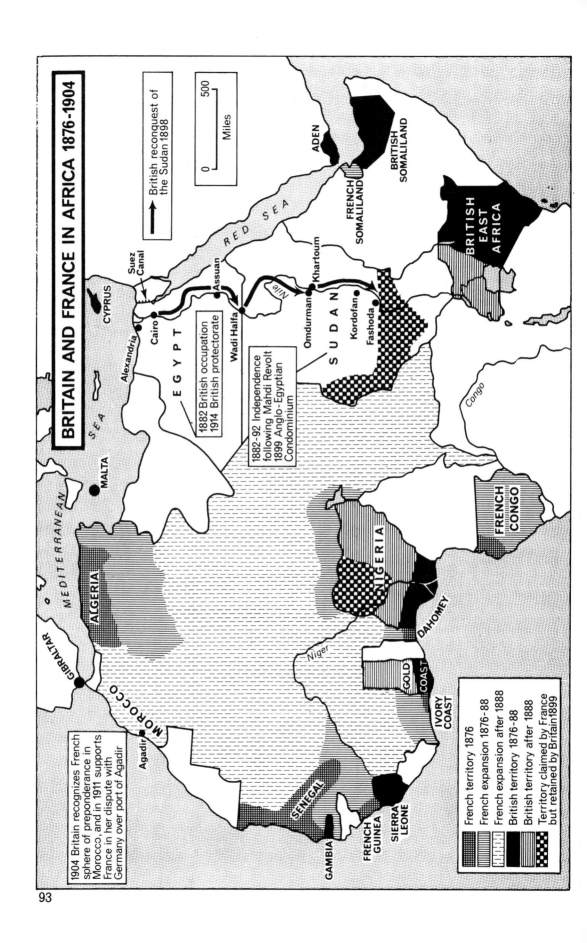

BRITAIN AND FRANCE IN AFRICA 1876-1904

British reconquest of
the Sudan 1898

500

Miles

0

ADEN

BRITISH
SOMALILAND

FRENCH
SOMALILAND

BRITISH
EAST
AFRICA

RED SEA

Suez
Canal

Khartoum

Assuan

Nile

Omdurman

Kordofan

Alexandria

Cairo

S U D A N

Fashoda

CYPRUS

Congo

E G Y P T

Wadi Halfa

1882 British occupation
1914 British protectorate

1882-92 Independence
following Mahdi Revolt
1899 Anglo-Egyptian
Condominium

MALTA

MEDITERRANEAN

S E A

FRENCH
CONGO

GIBRALTAR

ALGERIA

NIGERIA

DAHOMEY

Niger

GOLD
COAST

IVORY
COAST

MOROCCO

Agadir

SENEGAL

FRENCH
GUINEA

SIERRA
LEONE

GAMBIA

1904 Britain recognizes French
sphere of preponderance in
Morocco, and in 1911 supports
France in her dispute with
Germany over port of Agadir

French territory 1876

French expansion 1876-88

French expansion after 1888

British territory 1876-88

British territory after 1888

Territory claimed by France
but retained by Britain 1899

93

THE INDIAN EMPIRE IN 1901

RUSSIA

PERSIA

AFGHANISTAN

Kabul ○

Khyber Pass ○

NORTH WEST FRONTIER PROVINCE

CHITRAL

Peshawar ○

KASHMIR

BALUCHISTAN

B

CUTCH

PUNJAB

Lahore ○

Simla ○

Delhi ○

RAJPUTANA

SINDHIA

TIBET

NEPAL

SIKKIM

BHUTAN

Lhasa ○

CHINA

ASSAM

MANIPUR

BURMA

Rangoon ○

SIAM

UNITED PROVINCES

Lucknow ○

BENGAL

Calcutta ○

ORISSA

CENTRAL PROVINCES
AND BERAR

NIZAM'S
DOMINIONS

M A D R A S

B   A   Y

M

Bombay ○

MYSORE

Madras ○

TRAVANCORE

Indian States recognising Britain as the Paramount Power

Indian Provinces governed by British officials responsible
to the Viceroy of India

POPULATION IN 1901
British India 222,000,000
Indian States 67,000,000

0   400

Miles

BRITAIN AND RUSSIA IN CENTRAL ASIA 1870-1907

Russian expansion before 1870

British expansion after 1870

Russian expansion after 1870

British influence in Arabia after 1854

British protected areas

Russo-British buffer zone established by mutual agreement 1905 and given to Afghanistan

Russian sphere of influence in Persia 1907 (agreed with Britain)

British sphere of influence in Persia 1907 (agreed with Russia)

Younghusband's mission. Russian influence in Tibet is rebutted in 1904

Miles

0   500

TIBET

Lhasa

Gyantse

NEPAL

BHUTAN

1888

1871

CHINESE SINKIANG

1876

Tashkent

Samarkand

1895

1895

Srinagar

Lahore

Delhi

INDIA

Khyber Pass

Kabul

1891

Bokhara

1887

Quetta

1873

1884

1885

1887

Herat

AFGHANISTAN

Kandahar

1876

BALUCHISTAN

Karachi

1881

1893

Aral Sea

Meshed

INDIAN OCEAN

Caspian Sea

1873

Isfahan

PERSIA

Tiflis

Teheran

Bandar Abbas

OMAN

Kuria Muria Islands

1854

Tabriz

Kars

1878

Batum

Mosul

Baghdad

Basra

Kuwait 1899

Bahrein 1867

Persian Gulf

TRUCIAL STATES

1892

OTTOMAN EMPIRE

ARABIA

96

STRIKES AND RIOTS 1910–1912

July 1910. Railway strike.

Tyneside

September–December 1910. Boilermakers' strike.

December 1911. Strike of 126,000 weavers. Settled by a truce. One million pounds lost in wages.

September 1910. Cotton industry stoppage settled by Board of Trade.

Accrington

August 1911. Dockers' strike; riot quelled by troops. Two men killed.

Liverpool

November 1910. Riot during miners strike. Churchill delays army intervention. No deaths.

August 1911. Anti-Jewish violence by miners and tradesmen.

May 1912. Dock strike. Government refuse to intervene. Strike collapses after a month.

July 1912. Suffragette violence reaches peak in widespread destruction and burning of private property.

London

Llanelly

● Tredegar

Tonypandy

August 1911. Rioting during National rail strike. Two men shot dead by troops while looting shops and a train.

Southampton

June 1911. Ten day strike of seamen and firemen. The shipping magnates gave way, conceding all demands.

August 1911. Eleven day strike of 20,000 dockers. Settled to their satisfaction.

0   50

Miles

IRELAND 1914-1922

1916 Ireland exempt from conscription for duration of war.
1918 Sinn Fein establish independent Irish Parliament and refuse to send MP's to London.
1919-1921 The 'Troubles'. Guerilla warfare. About 750 Irish and 700 British dead.
1922 Irish Treaty establishes Irish Free State. British troops leave. Northern Ireland remains part of Great Britain
1936 Name changed to EIRE.
1948 Eire leaves British Commonwealth and becomes a Republic.

1914 Sinn Fein land weapons and ammunition illegally.

LONDONDERRY

ANTRIM
Larne

TYRONE

ULSTER
The Six Counties

FERMANAGH

DOWN

ARMAGH

1916 Easter rebellion. 450 Irish and 150 British killed. Irish Republic proclaimed: surrendered a week later.

1916 supports rebellion.

Dublin

1914 British officers 'mutiny' by refusing to contemplate fighting against Ulster.

Galway

Curragh

1916 Easter Monday rebellion against British rule crushed. Leaders executed 'A terrible beauty was born' (Yeats).

Enniscorthy

March 1916 Sir Roger Casement arrived from Germany. Arrested and shot for treason. He had tried to recruit Irish prisoners of war to fight against Britain.

Banna

1916 supports rebellion.

Wexford

March 1916 German ship with military aid for Sinn Fein intercepted by a British warship.

0   50
Miles

98

BRITISH DIPLOMACY 1904-1914

Guarantee of neutrality by Britain, France and Germany 1870. When Germany attacked Belgium in August 1914, Britain declared war on Germany.

Franco-Russian Alliance 1892.

Anglo-French Entente 1904 (military and naval conversations 1906-14).

Anglo-Russian Convention 1907. Colonial and territorial disputes settled.

The "Central Powers" 1914.

Associated with Britain, France & Russia following attack on them by Austria-Hungary.

Neutral at outbreak of war August 1914.

2 August 1914 Secret alliance with Germany.

28 July 1914 Austria attacks Serbia. 1 Aug.1914 Germany attacks France. 4 Aug.1914 Germany attacks Belgium. 4 August 1914 Britain declares war on Germany.

OTTOMAN EMPIRE

RUMANIA

BULGARIA

SERBIA

ALBANIA

GREECE

RUSSIA

AUSTRIA–HUNGARY

MONTENEGRO

ITALY

GERMANY

SWEDEN

NORWAY

DENMARK

HOLLAND

BELGIUM

SWITZERLAND

SARDINIA

SICILY

CORSICA

FRANCE

GREAT BRITAIN

SPAIN

PORTUGAL

Miles

0   300

THE FIRST WORLD WAR 1914-1918

MESOPOTAMIA March 1916 British success after 1915 initial setbacks.

PALESTINE British conquest October-December 1917.

ARABIA 1917 Successful Arab revolt supported by Britain. Lawrence of Arabia among British officers.

Russian gains March 1916-March1918. Retaken and held by Turks March to November 1918.

June 1916 Anglo-German naval battle confirmed British naval dominance in the North Sea but failed to destroy the German Fleet.

THE DARDANELLES British, Australian & New Zealand occupation April 1915-January 1916.Troops withdrawn when British Government felt it impossible to reach Constantinople. 46,000 Allied and 120,000 Turkish dead.

Baghdad

Jerusalem

Constantinople

T U R K E Y

Kharkov

Minsk

Riga

R O U M A N I A

AUSTRIA–HUNGARY

Belgrade

SERBIA

GREECE

ALBANIA

MONTENEGRO

Caporetto

Italian Front

G E R M A N Y

JUTLAND

SCAPA FLOW

Ypres

Paris

Western Front

Main British naval base

Front held by British troops

0 300 Miles

German and Austrian conquests 1914-1918

British, French and Russian conquests

Occupied by Germany after the treaty of Brest-Litovsk March-November 1918

Areas subject to frequent German air raids 1915-1918

British minefields

German minefields

MAIN BATTLES

1914 Oct-November FIRST YPRES German gains.
1915 March NEUVE CHAPELLE British gains.
1915 April-May SECOND YPRES British gains.
1915 September LOOS British gains.
1916 July-November SOMME British gains.
1917 April VIMY RIDGE Canadian gains.
1917 April-May ARRAS British gains.
1917 June MESSINES British gains.
1917 July-October THIRD YPRES British gains.
1917 November PASSCHENDAELE British gains.
1917 November CAMBRAI British gains.
1918 March-April {KEMMEL German gains
                 {SOMME German gains

Trench line by October 1914.

British gains.

German gains.

Main hospital areas

0   10
    Miles

COMMANDERS-IN-CHIEF
1914-1915 Sir John French.
1915-1918 Sir Douglas Haig.

St.Omer
1914-1915 Sir John French's headquarters.

FRANCE

Montreuil
1916-1918 Sir Douglas Haig's headquarters.

A million British and Empire soldiers died and three million were wounded in the shaded areas shown on this map.

Le Crotoy
St Valery
Headquarters of British lines of communication.
Abbeville

The Empire forces included Indians, South Africans, Canadians, Australians and New Zealanders. Manual labour behind the lines was done also by the Chinese Labour Corps and the South African Native Labour Corps.

Ostend

BELGIUM
BELGIAN ARMY
FLANDERS

Dunkirk

Calais

NORTHERN BOUNDARY BRITISH EXPEDITIONARY FORCE

Passchendaele
Ypres
Zonnebeke
Menin
Kemmel
Wytschaete
Messines
Bailleul
Ploegsteert
Armentieres
Bois Grenier
Lille

Cassel

Hazebrouck

ARTOIS

Boulogne

Neuve Chapelle
Aubers

Lillers
Béthune

Loos
Lens

Etaples

Vimy Ridge

St.Pol

Arras

Cambrai

Doullens

Bapaume

Thiepval

Albert

River Somme
Péronne

Amiens   FRENCH ARMY

SOUTHERN BOUNDARY BRITISH EXPEDITIONARY FORCE

THE WESTERN FRONT
1914-1918

INDUSTRIAL UNREST 1920–1939

Dundee

Glasgow
S

SCOTLAND

1924 First Labour Government
1926 General Strike, broken by
Conservative Government
1929–1931 Second Labour Government

Newcastle ⓢ Jarrow
TYNESIDE
✸ Durham

CUMBERLAND

LANCASHIRE ⓢⓢ YORKSHIRE
Liverpool ⓢ Sheffield

M I D L A N D S

SOUTH WALES
Swansea ⓢ
Merthyr ⓢ
ⓢ

London

May 1920 London dockers refuse to
load munitions on 'Jolly George'
for Polish defence against Russia

✸ Sabotage on railway lines by miners 1926
← Unemployed miners' hunger march 1936
▦ Area of heaviest unemployment (over 60%)
■ Serious unemployment
▨ Tythe payment resistance 1923
ⓢ Areas of frequent strike action:
South Wales 1920's
Lancashire 1930's
Glasgow early 1930's
Newcastle early 1920's, late 1930's

0 ___ 50
Miles

THE BRITISH EMPIRE 1920

In 1919 Britain acquired as Mandates the former German Colonies of Togo, Cameroon, Nauru, Tanganyika, German South West Africa (to South Africa) and Kaiser Wilhelm's Land (to Australia).

CANADA

THE UNITED KINGDOM OF GREAT BRITAIN AND IRELAND

NEWFOUNDLAND

GIBRALTAR

BERMUDA

•BAHAMAS

WEST INDIES
•BARBADOS
•TRINIDAD
JAMAICA

BRITISH HONDURAS

BRITISH GUIANA

GAMBIA

SIERRA LEONE

GOLD COAST

NIGERIA

CAMEROON

ASCENSION•

ST. HELENA•

TRISTAN DA CUNHA•

GOUGH ISLAND •

FALKLAND ISLANDS

SOUTH GEORGIA •

SANDWICH ISLANDS

SOUTH ORKNEYS

SOUTH SHETLANDS

GRAHAM LAND

PALESTINE

TRANSJORDAN

IRAQ

MALTA• CYPRUS

EGYPT

ANGLO-EGYPTIAN SUDAN

ADEN

SOCOTRA

BRITISH SOMALILAND

UGANDA

KENYA

TANGANYIKA (GERMAN EAST AFRICA)

NORTHERN RHODESIA

NYASALAND

SOUTHERN RHODESIA

BECHUANALAND

SOUTH WEST AFRICA

UNION OF SOUTH AFRICA

PRINCE EDWARD ISLAND

CROZET ISLAND•

SEYCHELLES

•CHAGOS
•DIEGO GARCIA

MAURITIUS

INDIA

BURMA

CEYLON

WEI HAI WEI

HONG KONG

MALAYA

BORNEO

KAISER WILHELM'S LAND

PAPUA

NAURU

GILBERT ISLANDS

ELLICE ISLANDS

FIJI•

NEW ZEALAND

AUSTRALIA

TASMANIA

BRITAIN AND THE MIDDLE EAST 1919-1967

TURKEY

GREECE

CRETE

MEDITERRANEAN SEA

CYPRUS
1960

LEBANON

SYRIA

British occupation 1941

PALESTINE
1948

TRANS
JORDAN
1946

CANAL
ZONE
(to Egypt)
1956

LIBYA

Occupied by
Britain 1943-1949

EGYPT
1922

ANGLO-EGYPTIAN
SUDAN
1956

MOsul

Kirkuk

IRAQ
1932

Basra

KUWAIT
1961

AFGHANISTAN

PAKISTAN
1947

PERSIA

1919-1921 War with Britain
1933 Frontier villages bombed

Anglo-Soviet occupation 1941-44

Ahwaz

PERSIAN GULF

Bahrein

QATAR

TRUCIAL STATES

MUSCAT & OMAN

SAUDI ARABIA

ADEN PROTECTORATE
1967

RED SEA

Kamaran
Island
1967
(to Aden)

YEMEN

Aden
1967

Perim Island 1967 (to Aden)

ETHIOPIA

1935.Appeals in vain
for help against Italy
1941. Britain active
in reconquest. The
Emperor restored

SOMALILAND
1960

INDIAN

OCEAN

Kuria Muria Islands
1967 (to Muscat)

Socotra

500

0

Miles

◄ British oil investments

▬ Oil pipelines

British mandates 1919, with dates
of independence

British protected territories

British possessions with dates
of independence

VIOLENCE IN INDIA 1919-1947

AFGHANISTAN

Police fire on mobs in 1919

KASHMIR

Peshawar
Gujranwala

Amritsar

PUNJAB

1922-1924 Reign of terror under Sikh Akhali sect

T I B E T

14 April 1920 Bombs dropped on Indian rioters

23 April 1930 Indian troops refuse British orders to fire on Indians

1922 Civil disobedience volunteers murder 21 policemen

N E P A L

UNITED PROVINCES

1919 British troops kill 379 unarmed Indians

GUJARAT

BIHAR

BENGAL

Police fire on mobs in 1919

I N D I A

Dandi

April-May 1930 Gandhi leads protest march against British salt monopoly

HYDERABAD

1944 Famine. 1,500,000 deaths

1921 Moplah rising. Violence against both Hindus and Europeans. 3,000 Moplahs killed.

MYSORE

TRAVANCORE

CEYLON

Indian violence against British rule 1919–1924

1924–1932

1937–1939

Violence and mass civil disobedience covered all India with the growth of the Quit India Movement in 1942

Hindu-Muslim riots both before and after the British left India in 1947 resulted in almost 2 million deaths

0   300
Miles

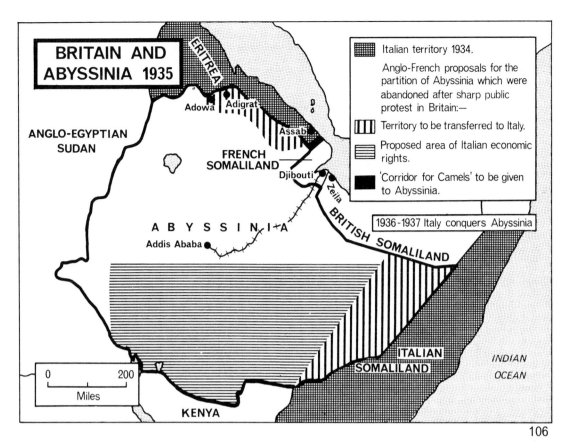

BRITAIN AND ABYSSINIA 1935

ERITREA

Adowa ● Adigrat

Assab ■

ANGLO-EGYPTIAN SUDAN

FRENCH SOMALILAND

Djibouti ●

Zeila

BRITISH SOMALILAND

A B Y S S I N I A

Addis Ababa ●

ITALIAN SOMALILAND

INDIAN OCEAN

KENYA

▦	Italian territory 1934.
	Anglo-French proposals for the partition of Abyssinia which were abandoned after sharp public protest in Britain:—
▥	Territory to be transferred to Italy.
▤	Proposed area of Italian economic rights.
■	'Corridor for Camels' to be given to Abyssinia.

1936-1937 Italy conquers Abyssinia

0 ——— 200
Miles

BRITAIN AND CZECHOSLOVAKIA 1938

GERMANY

Aussig ●
Brüx ●
Karlsbad ●
Saaz ●

Pilsen ●

Prague ●

C Z E C H O S L O V A K I A

BOHEMIA

MORAVIA

Brno ●

Teschen ●

POLAND

GERMANY (AUSTRIA)

Bratislava ●

SLOVAKIA

RUTHENIA

HUNGARY

◩	Czech territory ceded to Germany at Munich 30 September 1938 by Britain, France and Italy.
▢	Czech territory given to Hungary by Germany and Italy at Vienna 2 October 1938.
▨	Czech territory seized by Poland in September 1938 and formally annexed on 1 November 1938.
▦	Main Czech industrial and mineral resources transferred to Germany, Poland and Hungary.
◉	Frontier fortifications essential for Czech defence transferred to Germany.
+++	Main railways: lines of communication were broken by German occupied territory.

2,820,000 German speaking peoples, many opposed to Nazism, were transferred to Germany.

1,150,000 Czechs were put under German, Hungarian or Polish domination, and their minority rights ignored.

0 ——— 100
Miles

BRITISH DIPLOMACY 1939

Germany, her allies and associates, 3 Sept. 1939

Britain, her allies and associates 3 Sept.1939

Neutral states

August 1939 Russo-German Pact.

RUSSIA

TURKEY

ESTONIA

LATVIA

LITHUANIA

POLAND

March1939British guarantee. August1939British alliance.

ROUMANIA

April 1939 Anglo-French guarantee.

BULGARIA

GREECE

April1939 Anglo-French guarantee.

ALBANIA

YUGOSLAVIA

HUNGARY

SLOVAKIA

Free City of Danzig

SWEDEN

NORWAY

DENMARK

GERMANY

SWITZERLAND

Nov.1936 Pact of Steel with Germany.

ITALY

SARDINIA

CORSICA

SICILY

HOLLAND

BELGIUM

FRANCE

No formal alliance with Britain but co-operation on foreign policy and defence.

GREAT BRITAIN

EIRE

SPAIN

PORTUGAL

0   300
Miles

THE GERMAN THREAT TO BRITAIN 1939-1941

Legend:

- ⇨ German attacks April 1940
- British defensive positions April – May 1940. The last to resist was Narvik, until June 8.
- German occupied territory 10-24 May 1940
- Dunkirk perimeter 25-31 May 1940. By June 4 190,000 British and 140,000 French troops were rescued from the beaches. 100,000 allied troops were taken prisoner
- The Battle of Britain August – October 1940. British air mastery retained
- ◐ Towns severely bombed by the Germans 1940-41
- ▬ ▬ High altitude radar protection
- = = Low altitude radar protection
- States preserving their neutrality. The U.S.A. gave Britain substantial military aid 1939-41, while remaining neutral

Narvik

Bodo

Namsos

Andalsnes

Trondheim

SWEDEN

NORWAY
Surrendered 11 June 1940

Bergen

Oslo

DENMARK
Surrendered 9 April 1940

Copenhagen

Glasgow

EIRE

Hull

Liverpool

Manchester

Birmingham

Coventry

Bristol

London

Plymouth

Southampton Portsmouth

Dunkirk

CHANNEL ISLANDS
Occupied by Germans June 1940

G E R M A N Y

HOLLAND
Surrendered 15 May 1940

BELGIUM
Surrendered 28 May 1940

F R A N C E
•Paris
Surrendered 22 June 1940

SWITZERLAND

•Vichy

ITALY

0 _____ 500
Miles

THE DEFEAT OF GERMANY 1942-1945

GREENLAND

Occupied by
Britain 1941-1944

Archangel

ICELAND

▲ NORSE

▲ DANISH

NORTH

New York

AMERICA

DUTCH

Trieste

YUGOSLAV
ALBANIAN

FRENCH

GREEK

Casablanca

El Alamein

AFRICA

Dakar

SOUTH

AMERICA

Rio de Janeiro

Cape
Town

Montevideo

■	Under German rule or influence by December 1941
▨	Major German submarine activity 1941-1942
—	Principal allied convoy routes by 1943
●	Allied air bases by 1943
⟵	British forces active in the defeat of Germany 1942-1945
△	Partisan groups supported by Britain. Churchill's son Randolph fought with Yugoslav partisans

May 1944 to June 1945 the British reconquer Burma.
June 1945 U.S. troops liberate Borneo.
August 1945 the Japanese still hold Malaya at the time of their surrender.
1942-1945 the Americans reconquer the Pacific Islands and the Philippines.

BRITAIN AND JAPAN AT WAR 1941-1945

KOREA

Hiroshima
Nagasaki
JAPAN

CHINA

OKINAWA

BURMA

INDIA

FORMOSA

May 1942

HONG KONG
Surrendered
25 Dec 1941

Calcutta

THE PHILIPPINES
Surrendered
6 May 1942

Rangoon   Dec. 1941

THAILAND

FRENCH INDO-CHINA

Saigon

8 Dec 1941

NORTH BORNEO

BRUNEI

MALAYA

SINGAPORE
Surrendered
15 Feb. 1942

SARAWAK

DUTCH

EAST   INDIES

Japanese territory and conquests by November 1941.

British Empire never conquered by Japan.

Japanese advances December 1941-May 1942.

British Empire conquered by Japan by May 1942.

Furthest extent of Japanese conquest in S.E. Asia 1942-1943. In the Pacific the Japanese conquered the Gilbert and Ellice Islands but failed to reach Fiji.

Captured by U.S.A. May 1945 and used as a forward air base to bomb Southern Japan and Japanese-held China.

Atom bombs dropped by U.S.A., 6 and 9 August 1945. Over 110,000 Japanese civilian dead

AUSTRALIA

0   400
Miles

British occupation zones in Germany and Austria 1945–48.

European Free Trade Association (EFTA) 1958.

Associate Members of EFTA.

The "Iron Curtain".

European Common Market established by the Treaty of Rome 1957. Britain's first application in 1962 rejected. Second application made in 1967.

Members of the North Atlantic Treaty Organisation (NATO) established 1949. The USA and Canada are also members. Turkey was admitted 1951.

0   400
Miles

FINLAND
February 1947 Anglo–Soviet Peace Treaty limits Army to 34,000 men and Air Force to 60 machines.

SWEDEN

NORWAY

U. S. S. R.

DENMARK

EIRE

GREAT BRITAIN

NETHERLANDS

Berlin

POLAND

GERMAN DEMOCRATIC REPUBLIC

GERMAN FEDERAL REPUBLIC

CZECHOSLOVAKIA

BELGIUM

LUXEMBOURG

AUSTRIA

HUNGARY

RUMANIA

FRANCE

SWITZ.

ITALY

YUGOSLAVIA

BULGARIA

ALBANIA

PORTUGAL

SPAIN

GREECE

GIBRALTAR
Anglo–Spanish dispute over sovereignty

BRITAIN AND EUROPE 1945–1965

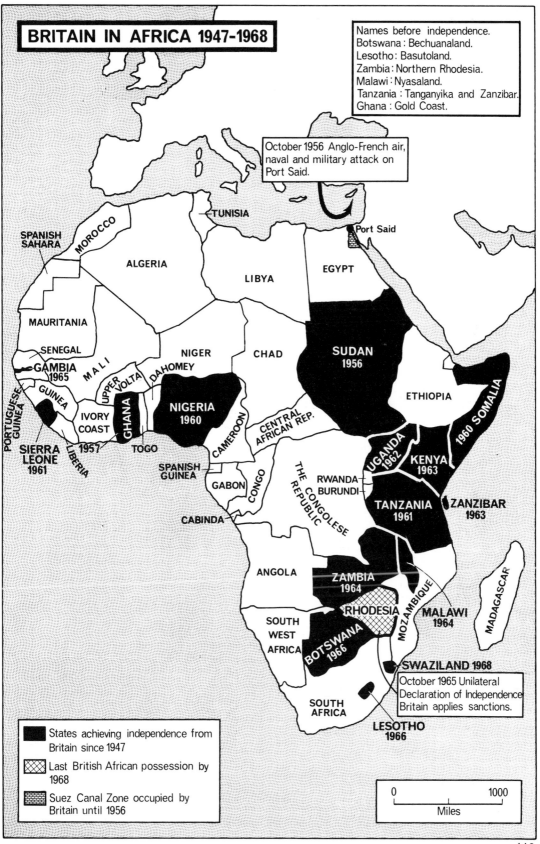

BRITAIN IN AFRICA 1947-1968

Names before independence.
Botswana : Bechuanaland.
Lesotho : Basutoland.
Zambia : Northern Rhodesia.
Malawi : Nyasaland.
Tanzania : Tanganyika and Zanzibar.
Ghana : Gold Coast.

October 1956 Anglo-French air, naval and military attack on Port Said.

SPANISH SAHARA

MOROCCO

TUNISIA

Port Said

ALGERIA

LIBYA

EGYPT

MAURITANIA

SENEGAL

GAMBIA 1965

MALI

NIGER

CHAD

SUDAN 1956

ETHIOPIA

1960 SOMALIA

GUINEA

PORTUGUESE GUINEA

SIERRA LEONE 1961

LIBERIA

IVORY COAST

GHANA

1957

UPPER VOLTA

DAHOMEY

TOGO

NIGERIA 1960

CAMEROON

CENTRAL AFRICAN REP.

UGANDA 1962

KENYA 1963

SPANISH GUINEA

GABON

CONGO

THE CONGOLESE REPUBLIC

RWANDA

BURUNDI

TANZANIA 1961

ZANZIBAR 1963

CABINDA

ANGOLA

ZAMBIA 1964

RHODESIA

MOZAMBIQUE

MALAWI 1964

MADAGASCAR

SOUTH WEST AFRICA

BOTSWANA 1966

SWAZILAND 1968

October 1965 Unilateral Declaration of Independence Britain applies sanctions.

SOUTH AFRICA

LESOTHO 1966

States achieving independence from Britain since 1947

Last British African possession by 1968

Suez Canal Zone occupied by Britain until 1956

0   1000
Miles

113

UNIVERSITY FOUNDATIONS 1264-1967

Aberdeen 1495

0   50
Miles

Dundee 1967
St. Andrews 1410
1967 Stirling
Glasgow 1451
Strathclyde 1964
Edinburgh 1583
Heriot-Watt 1966

Newcastle 1963
Durham 1832

Lancaster 1964
York 1963
Leeds 1904
Hull 1954
Bradford 1966
Liverpool 1903
Manchester 1851
Sheffield 1905
Salford 1967

Bangor
Keele 1962
Nottingham 1938
1966 Loughborough
Leicester 1957
East Anglia 1964

University of Wales 1893
Aston 1966
Birmingham 1900
Warwick 1965
Cambridge 1284
Aberystwyth

Essex 1965

Swansea
Oxford 1264
Cardiff
Brunel 1966
Reading 1926
Surrey 1966
London 1836
Bristol 1909
Kent 1965
Bath 1966
The City University 1966
Southampton 1952
Sussex 1961

Exeter 1955

● Founded 1264−1583
⊖ Nineteenth century foundations
◑ Founded 1900−1938
◉ Founded 1952−1967

114

BRITAIN 1945-1966

Legend:
- ▨ Continuous growth of population 1930-1960
- ▤ Continuous fall of population 1930-1960
- ● Towns where more than 10% of the population in private dwellings live two to a room (figures for 1958)
- ⊜ New towns built since 1945
- ◉ Oil Refineries 1966
- ◕ Nuclear Power Stations in operation by 1966
- ○ Drillings for Natural Gas 1964-1966
- ◎ Hydro-electric power stations

MAIN WAVES OF IMMIGRANTS

1880-1905	RUSSIAN JEWISH REFUGEES
1933-1939	GERMAN JEWISH REFUGEES
1956	HUNGARIAN REFUGEES
1956-1960	INDIAN, PAKISTANI AND WEST INDIAN IMMIGRANTS

POPULATION IN 1961: 50,368,455
of whom nearly 8 million in London area

North Sea

**Map labels:**
Dounreay, Cumbernauld, Glenrothes, Livingston, East Kilbride, Hunterston, Chapel Cross, Washington, Peterlee, Newton Aycliffe, Calder Hall, Springfields, Skelmersdale, Wylfa, Runcorn, Capenhurst, Trawsfynydd, Dawley, Corby, Sizewell, Stevenage, Hemel Hempstead, Welwyn, Harlow, Hatfield, Bradwell, Basildon, Milford Haven, Cwmbran, Berkeley, Oldbury, Bracknell, Crawley, Dungeness, Hinkley Point, Fawley

0 — 60 Miles

1945-1965 ROAD DEAD 121,797

THE BRITISH COMMONWEALTH 1967

CANADA

THE UNITED KINGDOM

JAMAICA

TRINIDAD AND TOBAGO

SIERRA LEONE

GUYANA

GAMBIA

GHANA

NIGERIA

MALTA

CYPRUS

UGANDA

KENYA

TANZANIA

MALAWI

ZAMBIA

BOTSWANA

LESOTHO

PAKISTAN

INDIA

CEYLON

MALAYSIA

SINGAPORE

AUSTRALIA

NEW ZEALAND

The Commonwealth is a free association of sovereign independent states, established at the Imperial Conference of 1926 and given legal status by the Statute of Westminster in 1931. In 1964 the total Commonwealth population was over 750 million.

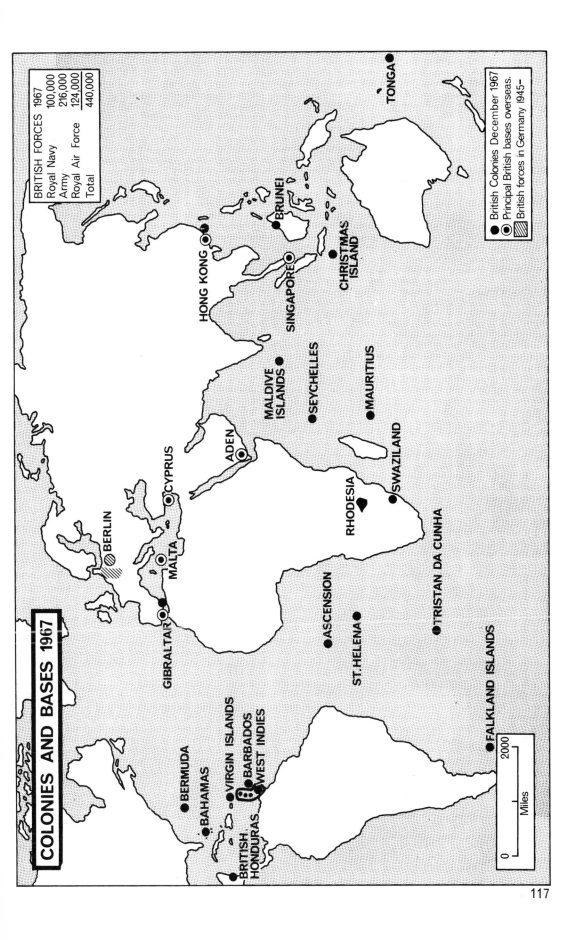

COLONIES AND BASES 1967

BRITISH FORCES 1967
Royal Navy	100,000
Army	216,000
Royal Air Force	124,000
Total	440,000

● British Colonies December 1967
◉ Principal British bases overseas.
▨ British forces in Germany 1945–

TONGA

BRUNEI

HONG KONG

SINGAPORE

CHRISTMAS ISLAND

MALDIVE ISLANDS

SEYCHELLES

MAURITIUS

ADEN

CYPRUS

SWAZILAND

BERLIN

RHODESIA

MALTA

GIBRALTAR

ASCENSION

ST. HELENA

TRISTAN DA CUNHA

BERMUDA

BAHAMAS

VIRGIN ISLANDS

BARBADOS

WEST INDIES

BRITISH HONDURAS

FALKLAND ISLANDS

0   2000
Miles

117

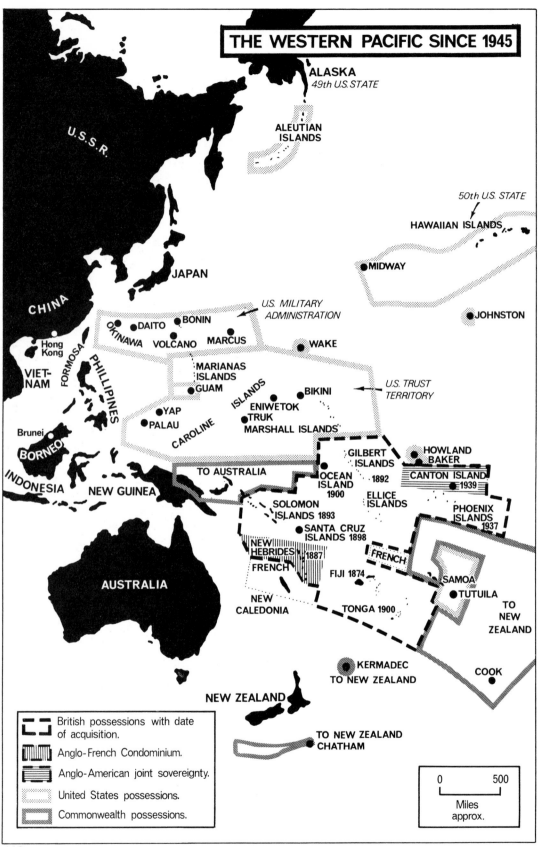

THE WESTERN PACIFIC SINCE 1945

ALASKA
49th U.S. STATE

U.S.S.R.

ALEUTIAN
ISLANDS

50th U.S. STATE

HAWAIIAN ISLANDS

MIDWAY

JAPAN

JOHNSTON

CHINA

*U.S. MILITARY
ADMINISTRATION*

DAITO · BONIN

OKINAWA
VOLCANO · MARCUS

WAKE

Hong
Kong

FORMOSA

PHILLIPINES

VIET-
NAM

MARIANAS
ISLANDS
GUAM

ISLANDS

BIKINI
ENIWETOK

*U.S. TRUST
TERRITORY*

YAP
PALAU

CAROLINE

TRUK
MARSHALL ISLANDS

Brunei

BORNEO

HOWLAND
BAKER

GILBERT
ISLANDS

CANTON ISLAND
1939

INDONESIA

NEW GUINEA

TO AUSTRALIA

OCEAN
ISLAND
1900

1892

ELLICE
ISLANDS

PHOENIX
ISLANDS
1937

SOLOMON
ISLANDS 1893

SANTA CRUZ
ISLANDS 1898

NEW
HEBRIDES 1887
FRENCH

AUSTRALIA

FRENCH

FIJI 1874

SAMOA

TUTUILA

NEW
CALEDONIA

TONGA 1900

TO
NEW
ZEALAND

KERMADEC
TO NEW ZEALAND

COOK

NEW ZEALAND

TO NEW ZEALAND
CHATHAM

British possessions with date
of acquisition.

Anglo-French Condominium.

Anglo-American joint sovereignty.

United States possessions.

Commonwealth possessions.

0   500

Miles
approx.

DISASTERS, 1952-1992

The advent of television put a greater focus than before on natural and man-made disasters. In some cases, such as the Bradford football stadium fire, the incident unfolded before the eyes of television viewers as it was taking place. This map shows, in black boxes, the numbers killed **2,288** in twenty-six disasters between 1952 and 1992. During the same period, **284,223** people were killed in road accidents

SHETLAND ISLANDS
45

2 November 1986, oil rig men in helicopter crash

6 July 1988, explosion and fire on an oil rig
166

124
27 March 1980, oil rig accommodation platform capsises

North Sea

2 January 1971, crush at a football stadium

21 December 1988, all 259 passengers and crew, and 11 people on the ground, killed when a terrorist bomb blew up a New York bound aircraft in flight

66 ●Glasgow

0 — kilometres — 100
0 — miles — 60

113

●Lockerbie
Stranraer
270

31 January 1953, ferry *Princess Victoria* sinks in a storm

23 May 1984, water-pumping station explodes

11 May 1985, fire engulfs soccer stadium grandstand

ISLE OF MAN
50
Douglas

1 June 1974, explosion in a chemical plant

Irish Sea

●Bowland
15   Bradford● ●Flixborough
56   ●Wakefield
Manchester●   **26**
54   Sheffield●
96

8 January 1989, damaged plane crashes while trying to land at East Midlands Airport

1 February 1953, East Coast storms

2 August 1973, fire at an amusement park

22 August 1985, plane burst into flames at airport

47
●Kegworth

307

8 October 1952, two express trains crash into a commuter train

7 March 1987, a British ferry, *Herald of Free Enterprise*, capsises

26 August 1984, food poisoning at a hospital

15 April 1989, football fans at Hillsborough Stadium killed when a crush barrier collapsed

●Aberfan
144

112 Harrow & Wealdstone●
Thames
King's Cross
●Moorgate
Clapham● ●St Johns

Zeebrugge●
188

BELGIUM

21 October 1966, 116 children among those killed in a school by an avalanche of coal, water, mud and rock

16 October 1987, hurricane

25 January 1990, hurricane

74
19
SOUTHERN ENGLAND

Brussels●
38

English Channel

29 May 1985, Heysel Stadium football riot involves British spectators

St Johns, 4 December 1957, **92** killed in commuter train crash
Moorgate, 28 February 1975, **41** killed in tube train crash
King's Cross, 18 November 1987, **31** killed during escalator fire
Clapham, 12 December 1988, **35** killed in commuter train crash
River Thames, 20 August 1989, **51** killed when a pleasure
　　steamer, the *Marchioness*, struck a barge

© Martin Gilbert 1993

119

OLD ENEMIES, NEW NATIONS: STATE VISITS 1955-1992

In addition to State and Commonwealth visits, the Queen has travelled extensively in Europe and the United States in both an official and a private capacity. In 1979 visited Saudi Arabia and the Gulf States. On 12 May 1992 she addressed the European Parliament in Strasbourg. She also regularly reviews British troops in Germany.

As Head of the Church of England, in 1961 the Queen made the first visit of a British Sovereign to the Vatican.

In 1945 Britain was part of the coalition which had defeated Germany, Italy and Japan. She was also a power with overseas possessions including the Indian Empire and large tracts of Africa. Forty years later the Empire was no more, and the defeated States were political allies and economic associates. The British Head of State, Queen Elizabeth II, made frequent visits to countries with which Britain had achieved, or with which she sought, good relations, including an ideological adversary, Communist China. This map shows States Visits from the first, in 1955, to 1992.

FEDERAL REPUBLIC OF GERMANY 1965 1978 1992

ITALY & VATICAN CITY 1961, 1980

Strasbourg

JAPAN 1975

SINGAPORE 1989

CHINA 1986

BANGLADESH 1983

THAILAND 1972

SRI LANKA 1981

INDONESIA 1974

NEPAL 1961 1986

INDIA 1983

IRAN 1961

MALDIVES 1972

AUSTRIA 1969

SWITZERLAND 1980

YUGOSLAVIA 1972

ETHIOPIA 1965

KENYA 1983

MALAWI 1979

ZIMBABWE 1991

BOTSWANA 1979

NORWAY 1955, 1981

FINLAND 1976

TURKEY 1971

JORDAN 1984

SUDAN 1965

TANZANIA 1979

ZAMBIA 1979

NAMIBIA 1991

ICELAND 1990

SWEDEN 1956 1983

DENMARK 1957 1979

NETHERLANDS 1958

BELGIUM 1966

LUXEMBOURG 1976

FRANCE 1957 1992

SPAIN 1988

PORTUGAL 1957 1985

MOROCCO 1980

MALTA 1992

ALGERIA 1980

TUNISIA 1980

LIBERIA 1961

North Atlantic Ocean

South Atlantic Ocean

Pacific Ocean

BRAZIL 1968

UNITED STATES 1957 1976 1991

MEXICO 1975

CHILE 1968

Pacific Ocean

© Martin Gilbert, 1993

121

BRITAIN AND EUROPE, 1957-1993

On 25 March 1957 the Treaty of Rome established a European Economic Community (the EEC or Common Market) of six nations. Britain entered on 22 January 1972. On 7 February 1992 the Treaty of Maastricht accepted the move towards future common foreign and defence policies, and a single currency for 1999, (with Britain able to "opt out" if she wished). On 12 December 1992, at Edinburgh, it was agreed that each member State would pay some 1.28% of its gross national product to the Community finances. On 1 January 1993 the establishment of a Single European Market brought an end to tariff barriers among the twelve member States

The German Democratic Republic (East Germany) was joined to the Federal Republic (West Germany) in October 1991, with Berlin as the capital of the united Germany

On 12 September 1991 John Major proposed the extension of full membership of the European Community to the States of Eastern Europe, and eventually to the Soviet Republics (from December 1991, the Commonwealth of Independent States)

The European Community accounted in 1992 for one fifth of all world trade. Half of Britain's world trade in 1992 was with the other eleven members of the Community

SOVIET UNION
(COMMONWEALTH OF INDEPENDENT STATES from 21 December 1991)

Original member States of the European Community, 1957

States joining in 1972

States joining after 1972, with dates

States with whom, as a result of the Edinburgh Summit decisions, negotiations for entry were to begin

© Martin Gilbert, 1993

122

NORTHERN IRELAND, 1969-1993

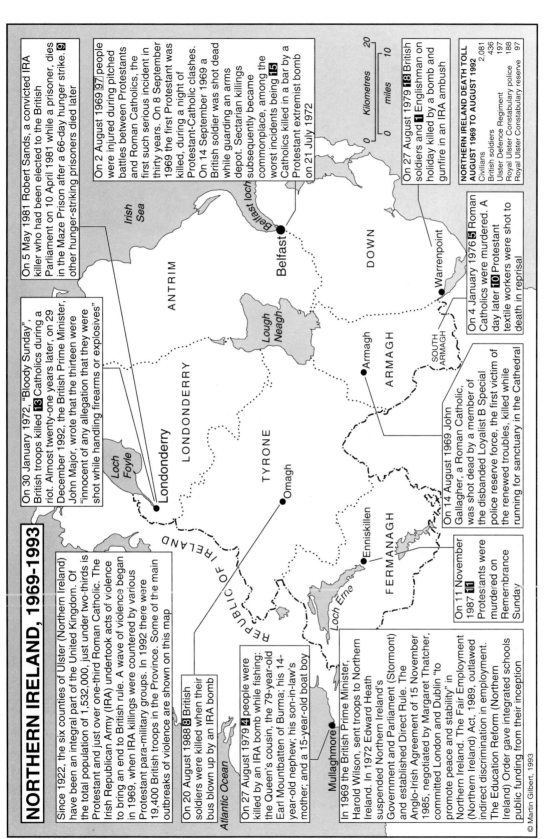

Since 1922, the six counties of Ulster (Northern Ireland) have been an integral part of the United Kingdom. Of the total population of 1,532,000, just under two-thirds is Protestant and just over one-third Roman Catholic. The Irish Republican Army (IRA) undertook acts of violence to bring an end to British rule. A wave of violence began in 1969, when IRA killings were countered by various Protestant para-military groups. In 1992 there were 19,400 British troops in the Province. Some of the main outbreaks of violence are shown on this map

On 5 May 1981 Robert Sands, a convicted IRA killer who had been elected to the British Parliament on 10 April 1981 while a prisoner, dies in the Maze Prison after a 66-day hunger strike. 9 other hunger-striking prisoners died later

On 2 August 1969 97 people were injured during pitched battles between Protestants and Roman Catholics, the first such serious incident in thirty years. On 8 September 1969 the first Protestant was killed, during a night of Protestant-Catholic clashes. On 14 September 1969 a British soldier was shot dead while guarding an arms depot. Sectarian killings subsequently became commonplace, among the worst incidents being 15 Catholics killed in a bar by a Protestant extremist bomb on 21 July 1972

On 30 January 1972, "Bloody Sunday", British troops killed 13 Catholics during a riot. Almost twenty-one years later, on 29 December 1992, the British Prime Minister, John Major, wrote that the thirteen were "innocent of any allegation that they were shot while handling firearms or explosives"

On 27 August 1979 18 British soldiers and 1 Englishman on holiday killed by a bomb and gunfire in an IRA ambush

On 20 August 1988 8 British soldiers were killed when their bus blown up by an IRA bomb

On 27 August 1979 4 people were killed by an IRA bomb while fishing: the Queen's cousin, the 79-year-old Earl Mountbatten of Burma; his 14-year-old nephew; his son-in-law's mother; and a 15-year-old boat boy

In 1969 the British Prime Minister, Harold Wilson, sent troops to Northern Ireland. In 1972 Edward Heath suspended Northern Ireland's Government and Parliament (Stormont) and established Direct Rule. The Anglo-Irish Agreement of 15 November 1985, negotiated by Margaret Thatcher, committed London and Dublin "to promote peace and stability" in Northern Ireland. The Fair Employment (Northern Ireland) Act, 1989, outlawed indirect discrimination in employment. The Education Reform (Northern Ireland) Order gave integrated schools public funding from their inception

On 11 November 1987 11 Protestants were murdered on Remembrance Sunday

On 14 August 1969 John Gallagher, a Roman Catholic, was shot dead by a member of the disbanded Loyalist B Special police reserve, the first victim of the renewed troubles, killed while running for sanctuary in the Cathedral

On 4 January 1976 5 Roman Catholics were murdered. A day later 10 Protestant textile workers were shot to death in reprisal

NORTHERN IRELAND DEATH TOLL AUGUST 1969 TO AUGUST 1992

Civilians	2,081
British soldiers	436
Ulster Defence Regiment	197
Royal Ulster Constabulary police	188
Royal Ulster Constabulary reserve	97

Londonderry
Belfast
Armagh
Omagh
Enniskillen
Warrenpoint
Mullaghmore

ANTRIM
DOWN
LONDONDERRY
TYRONE
ARMAGH
SOUTH ARMAGH
FERMANAGH

Irish Sea
Belfast loch
Lough Neagh
Loch Foyle
Loch Erne

Atlantic Ocean

REPUBLIC OF IRELAND

0 Kilometres 10 20
0 miles 10

© Martin Gilbert, 1993

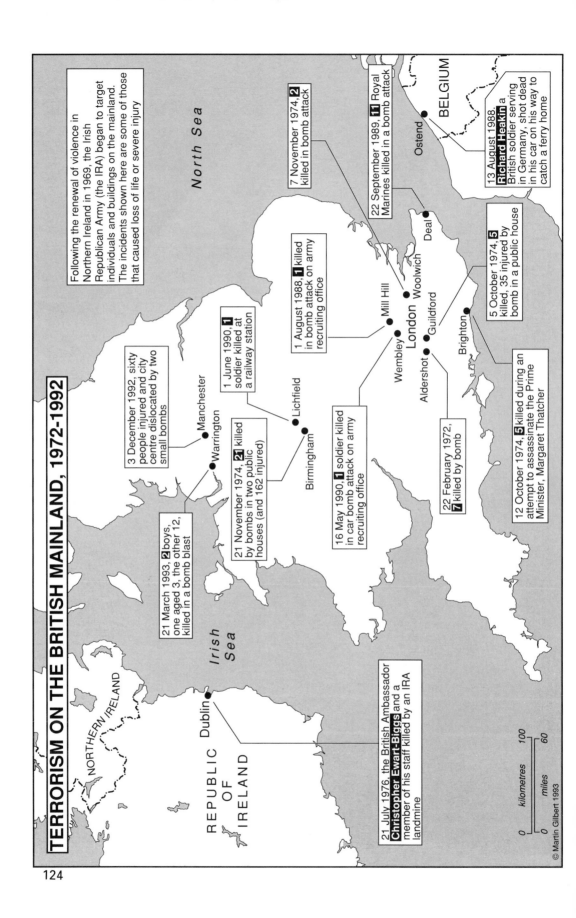

TERRORISM ON THE BRITISH MAINLAND, 1972-1992

Following the renewal of violence in Northern Ireland in 1969, the Irish Republican Army (the IRA) began to target individuals and buildings on the mainland. The incidents shown here are some of those that caused loss of life or severe injury

North Sea

7 November 1974, **2** killed in bomb attack

22 September 1989, **11** Royal Marines killed in a bomb attack

13 August 1988, **Richard Heakin** a British soldier serving in Germany, shot dead in his car on his way to catch a ferry home

BELGIUM

Ostend

Deal

1 August 1988, **1** killed in bomb attack on army recruiting office

Mill Hill

Woolwich

London

Wembley

Guildford

Aldershot

Brighton

5 October 1974, **5** killed, 35 injured by bomb in a public house

3 December 1992, sixty people injured and city centre dislocated by two small bombs

1 June 1990, **1** soldier killed at a railway station

Manchester

Warrington

Lichfield

Birmingham

21 November 1974, **21** killed by bombs in two public houses (and 162 injured)

16 May 1990, **1** soldier killed in car bomb attack on army recruiting office

22 February 1972, **7** killed by bomb

12 October 1974, **5** killed during an attempt to assassinate the Prime Minister, Margaret Thatcher

21 March 1993, **2** boys, one aged 3, the other 12, killed in a bomb blast

Irish Sea

NORTHERN IRELAND

Dublin

REPUBLIC OF IRELAND

21 July 1976, the British Ambassador **Christopher Ewart-Biggs** and a member of his staff killed by an IRA landmine

0   kilometres   100

0   miles   60

© Martin Gilbert 1993

124

TERRORISM IN LONDON, 1973–1992

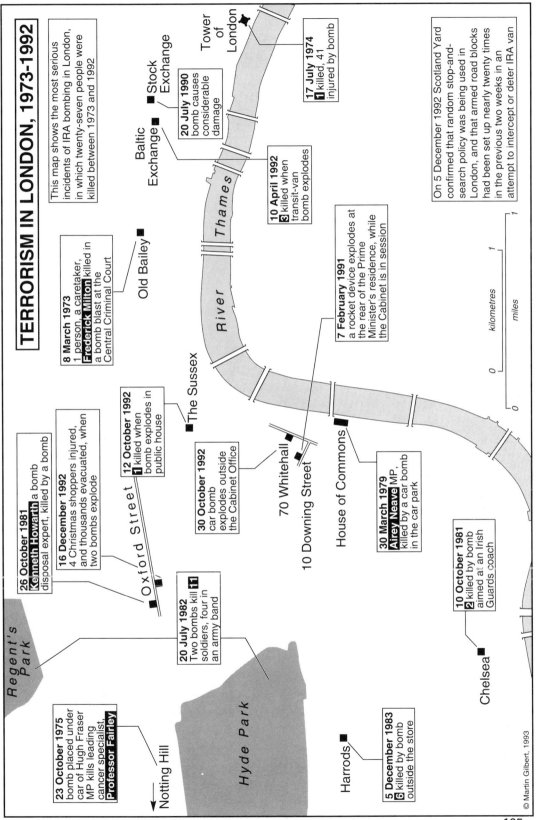

This map shows the most serious incidents of IRA bombing in London, in which twenty-seven people were killed between 1973 and 1992

8 March 1973
1 person, a caretaker, **Frederick Milton** killed in a bomb blast at the Central Criminal Court

■ Old Bailey

26 October 1981
Kenneth Howarth a bomb disposal expert, killed by a bomb

16 December 1992
4 Christmas shoppers injured, and thousands evacuated, when two bombs explode

12 October 1992
1 killed when bomb explodes in public house

■ The Sussex

30 October 1992
car bomb explodes outside the Cabinet Office

Oxford Street

20 July 1982
Two bombs kill **1** soldiers, four in an army band

Regent's Park

23 October 1975
bomb placed under car of Hugh Fraser MP kills leading cancer specialist, **Professor Fairley**

Notting Hill

Hyde Park

5 December 1983
6 killed by bomb outside the store

Harrods ■

Baltic Exchange ■

Stock Exchange ■

20 July 1990
bomb causes considerable damage

Tower of London

17 July 1974
1 killed, 41 injured by bomb

10 April 1992
3 killed when transit-van bomb explodes

River Thames

7 February 1991
a rocket device explodes at the rear of the Prime Minister's residence, while the Cabinet is in session

70 Whitehall

10 Downing Street

House of Commons ■

30 March 1979
Airey Neave MP, killed by a car bomb in the car park

10 October 1981
2 killed by bomb aimed at an Irish Guards coach

Chelsea ■

On 5 December 1992 Scotland Yard confirmed that random stop-and-search policy was being used in London, and that armed road blocks had been set up nearly twenty times in the previous two weeks in an attempt to intercept or deter IRA van

0   kilometres   1

0   miles   1

© Martin Gilbert, 1993

NORTH SEA GAS AND OIL SINCE 1967

Oil The discovery of oil in the North Sea, and its production from 1975, gave Britain a major extra natural resource, and an important source of income, at a time of rapidly rising oil prices worldwide. With an average output of 2.6 million barrels a day, Britain became the world's sixth largest oil producer

By the end of 1989 there were forty-four off-shore fields producing crude oil. That year, the Government approved a further thirteen off-shore development projects. Production is forecast to decline slowly, but to enable Britain to be self sufficient in oil until the end of the century, and a significant producer of oil in the twenty-first century

Gas From 1967, natural gas supplies from the North Sea were sufficient to replace hitherto coal-based supplies of town gas. By 1989 twenty-eight North Sea fields were in operation. Distribution was through a network of 11,100 miles (17,600 kilometres) of pipes. Eighty percent of natural gas consumed in Britain comes from the British North Sea fields; the remainder comes from Norwegian fields

Under the Gas Act 1986, the British Gas Corporation, in State ownership since 1949, was privatised, and its assets transferred to British Gas plc, which in 1989 had two-and-a-half million shareholders and 79,000 employees. Almost half of the gas supplied is for industrial and commercial use, and just over half is for household consumption

Magnus
Emerald
Ninian
Sullom Voe
NORWAY
SHETLAND ISLANDS
Frigg
ORKNEY ISLANDS
Flotta
St Fergus
Forties
Gannet
Ekofisk
North Sea
Grangemouth
North Tees
Teesside
Dimlington
Barrow
Buoy
Easington
Killingholme
Indefatigable
Stanlow
Theddlethorpe
Bacton
Milford Haven
Canvey
Shellhaven
Coryton
Pembroke
Angle Bay
Fawley

- ● off-shore oil-fields
- ◉ crude oil terminals
- - - main crude oil pipelines
- ● oil refineries (refining more than 1 million tonnes annually)

- △ major natural gas fields
- ▲ major natural gas terminals
- = major natural gas pipelines

0 kilometres 100
0 miles 60

© Martin Gilbert, 1993

126

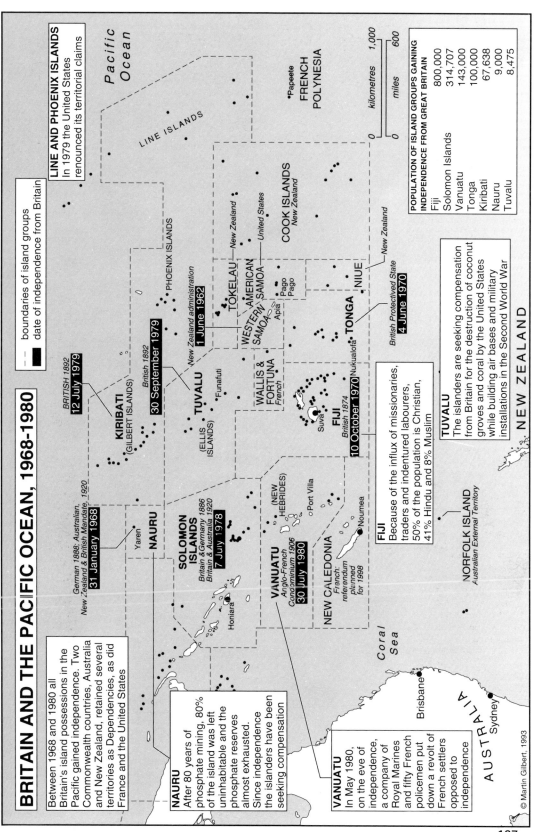

BRITAIN AND THE PACIFIC OCEAN, 1968-1980

Between 1968 and 1980 all Britain's island possessions in the Pacific gained independence. Two Commonwealth countries, Australia and New Zealand, retained several territories as Dependencies, as did France and the United States

--- boundaries of island groups

▬ date of independence from Britain

LINE AND PHOENIX ISLANDS
In 1979 the United States renounced its territorial claims

Pacific Ocean

LINE ISLANDS

Papeete FRENCH POLYNESIA

kilometres		1,000
0		
miles		600
0		

POPULATION OF ISLAND GROUPS GAINING INDEPENDENCE FROM GREAT BRITAIN	
Fiji	800,000
Solomon Islands	314,707
Vanuatu	143,000
Tonga	100,000
Kiribati	67,638
Nauru	9,000
Tuvalu	8,475

PHOENIX ISLANDS

British 1892
KIRIBATI
(GILBERT ISLANDS)
12 July 1979

TUVALU
(ELLIS ISLANDS)
30 September 1979
British 1892
Funafuti

COOK ISLANDS
New Zealand

TOKELAU *New Zealand*
New Zealand administration
1 June 1962

WESTERN
AMERICAN
SAMOA
Apia *United States*
Pago Pago

WALLIS & FORTUNA
French

NIUE
New Zealand

TONGA
Nukualofa
British Protected State
4 June 1970

FIJI
British 1874
Suva
10 October 1970

German 1888; Australian, New Zealand & British Mandate, 1920
NAURU
Yaren
31 January 1968

SOLOMON ISLANDS
*Britain &Germany 1886
Britain & Australia 1920*
Honiara
7 July 1978

VANUATU
Anglo-French Condominium 1906
(NEW HEBRIDES)
Port Villa
30 July 1980

NEW CALEDONIA
French: referendum planned for 1998
Noumea

TUVALU
The islanders are seeking compensation from Britain for the destruction of coconut groves and coral by the United States while building air bases and military installations in the Second World War

FIJI
Because of the influx of missionaries, traders and indentured labourers, 50% of the population is Christian, 41% Hindu and 8% Muslim

NORFOLK ISLAND
Australian External Territory

NAURU
After 80 years of phosphate mining, 80% of the island was left uninhabitable and the phosphate reserves almost exhausted. Since independence the islanders have been seeking compensation

VANUATU
In May 1980, on the eve of independence, a company of Royal Marines and fifty French policemen put down a revolt of French settlers opposed to independence

Coral Sea

NEW ZEALAND

Brisbane

AUSTRALIA
Sydney

© Martin Gilbert, 1993

ASYLUM, 1985–1992

Britain is a signatory of the 1951 United Nations Convention on Refugees, under which asylum should be granted to any refugee "with a well-founded fear of being persecuted for reasons of race, religion, nationality, membership of a particular social group, or political opinion"

Among groups helping refugees are, nationally, the United Kingdom Refugee Council, and, locally, groups such as the Newham Monitoring Project (London), the Southall Monitoring Group (London), and the Sheffield Somali Refugees Trust

On 4 March 1992 a Sudanese man who fled from racist attacks in Germany was granted political asylum in Britain on the grounds of a "well-founded fear of persecution in Germany"

In early November 1992 the British Government announced it would take 600 refugees from Bosnia. Following pressure from refugee-support groups, it was announced on 1 December 1992 that a further 3,400 Bosnian refugees would be admitted. In addition, 40,000 people from the former Yugoslav republics had been accepted as visitors in 1992

The only country in the Americas from which refugees were granted asylum to Britain between 1985 and 1992 was Colombia: 31 admitted

Between 1984 and 1988 a total of 998,000 Britons emigrated, to live abroad. In that same period, 1,100,000 people came from overseas to live in Britain (a net population increase of 114,000)

In addition to 2,400 people granted asylum in 1990, more than 28,000 individuals were permitted to immigrate to Britain

PRINCIPAL IMMIGRATION TO BRITAIN, 1990

India, Pakistan, Bangladesh	12,980
Australia, New Zealand	5,170
United States	3,660
Middle East (Arab lands)	2,980
European Community	1,760
Stateless refugees	1,400
Canada	850
Eastern Europe	630

■ number of refugees granted asylum, 1985 to 1992, shown by country of orgin

SOVIET UNION 65

RUMANIA 27

BULGARIA 27

TURKEY 2,038

LEBANON 480

NIGERIA 10

GHANA 1,684

ANGOLA 78

ZAIRE 167

SUDAN 101

IRAQ 969

IRAN 2,841

ETHIOPIA 1,053

SOMALIA 1,791

UGANDA 1,443

PAKISTAN 200

INDIA 175

CHINA 89

SRI LANKA 5,443

London

Sheffield

© Martin Gilbert, 1993

128

ETHNIC MINORITIES, 1991

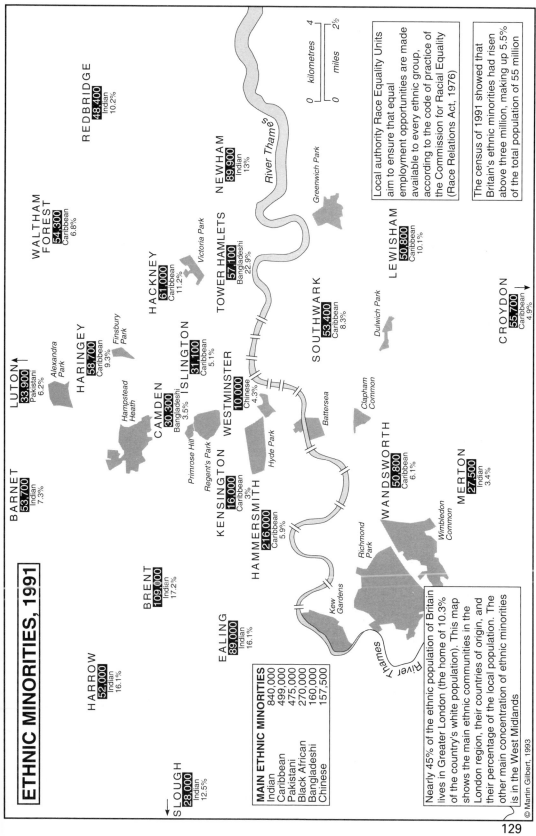

MAIN ETHNIC MINORITIES

Indian	840,000
Caribbean	499,000
Pakistani	475,000
Black African	270,000
Bangladeshi	160,000
Chinese	157,500

Nearly 45% of the ethnic population of Britain lives in Greater London (the home of 10.3% of the country's white population). This map shows the main ethnic communities in the London region, their countries of origin, and their percentage of the local population. The other main concentration of ethnic minorities is in the West Midlands

© Martin Gilbert, 1993

Local authority Race Equality Units aim to ensure that equal employment opportunities are made available to every ethnic group, according to the code of practice of the Commission for Racial Equality (Race Relations Act, 1976)

The census of 1991 showed that Britain's ethnic minorities had risen above three million, making up 5.5% of the total population of 55 million

SLOUGH 28,000 Indian 12.5%

HARROW 52,000 Indian 16.1%

BRENT 109,000 Indian 17.2%

EALING 89,000 Indian 16.1%

BARNET 53,700 Indian 7.3%

LUTON 33,900 Pakistani 6.2%

HARINGEY 58,700 Caribbean 9.3%

CAMDEN 30,300 Bangladeshi 3.5%

WALTHAM FOREST 54,300 Caribbean 6.8%

REDBRIDGE 48,400 Indian 10.2%

HACKNEY 61,000 Caribbean 11.2%

ISLINGTON 31,100 Caribbean 5.1%

WESTMINSTER 10,000 Chinese 4.3%

TOWER HAMLETS 57,100 Bangladeshi 22.9%

NEWHAM 89,900 Indian 13%

KENSINGTON 16,000 Caribbean 3%

HAMMERSMITH 216,000 Caribbean 5.9%

SOUTHWARK 53,400 Caribbean 8.3%

LEWISHAM 50,800 Caribbean 10.1%

WANDSWORTH 50,800 Caribbean 6.1%

MERTON 27,500 Indian 3.4%

CROYDON 55,700 Caribbean 4.9%

Alexandra Park

Finsbury Park

Hampstead Heath

Primrose Hill

Regent's Park

Hyde Park

Victoria Park

Greenwich Park

Battersea

Clapham Common

Dulwich Park

Richmond Park

Wimbledon Common

Kew Gardens

River Thames

River Thames

kilometres 0 ... 4

miles 0 ... 2½

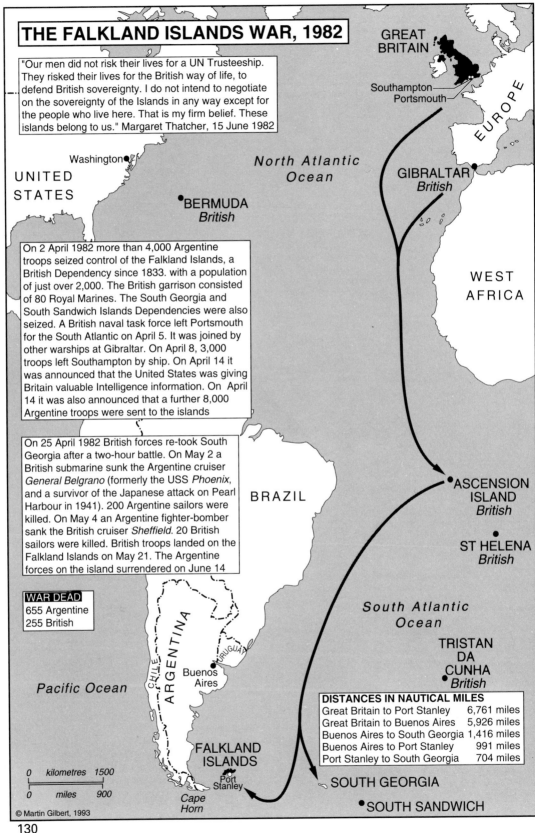

THE FALKLAND ISLANDS WAR, 1982

"Our men did not risk their lives for a UN Trusteeship. They risked their lives for the British way of life, to defend British sovereignty. I do not intend to negotiate on the sovereignty of the Islands in any way except for the people who live here. That is my firm belief. These islands belong to us." Margaret Thatcher, 15 June 1982

GREAT BRITAIN

Southampton
Portsmouth

Washington

UNITED STATES

North Atlantic Ocean

GIBRALTAR
British

EUROPE

BERMUDA
British

WEST AFRICA

On 2 April 1982 more than 4,000 Argentine troops seized control of the Falkland Islands, a British Dependency since 1833. with a population of just over 2,000. The British garrison consisted of 80 Royal Marines. The South Georgia and South Sandwich Islands Dependencies were also seized. A British naval task force left Portsmouth for the South Atlantic on April 5. It was joined by other warships at Gibraltar. On April 8, 3,000 troops left Southampton by ship. On April 14 it was announced that the United States was giving Britain valuable Intelligence information. On April 14 it was also announced that a further 8,000 Argentine troops were sent to the islands

On 25 April 1982 British forces re-took South Georgia after a two-hour battle. On May 2 a British submarine sunk the Argentine cruiser *General Belgrano* (formerly the USS *Phoenix*, and a survivor of the Japanese attack on Pearl Harbour in 1941). 200 Argentine sailors were killed. On May 4 an Argentine fighter-bomber sank the British cruiser *Sheffield*. 20 British sailors were killed. British troops landed on the Falkland Islands on May 21. The Argentine forces on the island surrendered on June 14

BRAZIL

ASCENSION ISLAND
British

ST HELENA
British

South Atlantic Ocean

WAR DEAD
655 Argentine
255 British

CHILE
ARGENTINA
URUGUAY
Buenos Aires

TRISTAN DA CUNHA
British

Pacific Ocean

DISTANCES IN NAUTICAL MILES
Great Britain to Port Stanley	6,761 miles
Great Britain to Buenos Aires	5,926 miles
Buenos Aires to South Georgia	1,416 miles
Buenos Aires to Port Stanley	991 miles
Port Stanley to South Georgia	704 miles

FALKLAND ISLANDS

Port Stanley

0   kilometres   1500
0   miles   900

© Martin Gilbert, 1993

Cape Horn

SOUTH GEORGIA

SOUTH SANDWICH

BRITAIN, THE GULF WAR AND ITS AFTERMATH, 1990-1993

On 2 August 1990 Iraqi forces occupied Kuwait. The United Nations Security Council demanded immediate withdrawal. On 29 November 1990 the Security Council authorised UN members to use force to expel Iraq from Kuwait. On 17 January 1991 Allied air forces, British among them, attacked strategic targets throughout Iraq and Iraqi-occupied Kuwait. On 24 February 1991 British forces participated in the land offensive. Four days later Iraq announced a cease-fire

Following the Gulf War, Iraqi forces killed an estimated 30,000 Kurds in the north and Sh'ite Muslims in the south. On 6 April 1991 Britain and the United States warned Iraq not to send warplanes north of the 32nd parallel. Iraq complied. On 17 April 1991 US, British and French troops crossed into northern Iraq to secure "Safe Havens" for the Kurds, and to construct refugee camps

Of the 25,000 British troops who took part in the Gulf War 24 were killed in action

On 27 August 1992 the United States established a "No-Fly Zone" in the south. With the agreement of Britain and France, Iraqi warplanes flying south of the 36th parallel would be shot down from 7 January 1993. United States, British and French warplanes were subsequently in action against Iraqi anti-aircraft batteries

➤ British forces in action, January-February 1991

✳ British commandos active behind the lines, seeking out and destroying scud missile launchers, January-February 1991

▨ Safe Havens established for the Kurds

◉ Iraqi anti-aircraft batteries attacked, 13-18 January 1993

© Martin Gilbert 1993

131

HOMELESSNESS, 1977-1993

"It is not an exaggeration to say that most homeless people can pick up three Christmas dinners a day at this time of year. We have to make people realise that the homeless are with us all year." (John Evans, Edinburgh Council for the Single Homeless, Christmas 1992)

Open Door provides eight-week training projects for 16 and 17-year-old unemployed, and those in temporary accommodation

Under the Homeless Persons Act 1977, local councils have a statutory duty to investigate the circumstances of the homeless, and to determine their priority needs. With unemployment going above 3 million in 1993, the problem of homeless families became acute. Tens of thousands of families with mortgages were forced by economic hardship to give up their homes. By December 1992, 450,000 people were registered as homeless, of whom 15,000 had become homeless that year. In London, in January 1993, 114,000 individuals were registered as homeless, with up to 3,000 sleeping rough each night

81,738	Households accepted as homeless by local authorities, 1981
187,265	Households accepted as homeless by local authorities, 1991
57.737	families in bed & breakfast hotels and hostels, 1991

Under the slogan "helping the homeless to help themselves", the London homeless publish a fortnightly magazine, *The Big Issue*, of which 60% of the cover price goes to the homeless person selling it. The 22 January 1993 number contains a note: "Vendor 986 (Mark) wishes to thank all his customers, particularly the people of Ealing Broadway, for their generous support over recent months. Mark now has a full-time job working for *The Big Issue* Outreach Team and has secured accommodation"

Crisis, a charity for the homeless, opened five 24-hour centres for the homeless in the North-West, and three in London, over Christmas 1992

SCOTLAND
8,149
31,709

Glasgow   Edinburgh

NORTH
3,626
8,990
570

YORKSHIRE & HUMBERSIDE
5,747
12,660
1,750

NORTH WEST
6,853
23,890
2,200

EAST MIDLANDS
4,879
9,880
1,770

WEST MIDLANDS
8,969
18,350
2,110

EAST ANGLIA
1,744
3,700
1,070

WALES
5,462
9,766
577

SOUTH EAST & GREATER LONDON
30,128
59,020
47,690
● London

| 0 | kilometres | 100 |
| 0 | miles | 60 |

SOUTH WEST
6,181
9,300

MORTGAGE REPOSSESSIONS	
1989	15,810
1990	43,890
1991	75,000
1992	68,000

© Martin Gilbert 1993

132

HOMES FOR THE HOMELESS, 1992-1993

This map shows towns in which the Sutton Housing Trust (founded in 1894) was renting, at the beginning of 1993, more than 14,000 low cost homes, being committed to "the relief of persons with low income resident in England who are in conditions of need by the provision of housing and hostels"

Among charities and organisations helping the homeless are: Shelter, Crisis, The London Housing Aid Centre (SHAC), the Campaign for Single Homeless People (CHAR), the Camden Training and Homeless Youth Forum (CATHY), the Department of Employment's Homeless Employment in London Project (HELP), and the Industrial Society's Linked Employment Accommodation Project (LEAP)

On 28 November 1992 the Department of the Environment announced that it would make available £577 million to buy up 16,000 homes to house the homeless. The main provider of these homes are 2,326 registered Housing Associations. By 8 December 1992, one of these, the Bedfordshire Pilgrims Housing Association, had spent its total allocation (£3.7million) on the purchase of 110 properties

In 1993 Bedford Borough Council appointed a Senior Homelessness and Housing Advice Officer, responsible for "a high volume of homelessness cases"

A voluntary organisation, the Cyrenians, funded by local government and private charity, provides supportive housing. Outreach workers are provided for those sleeping rough, for health care, mental health care, and a day centre

London Rough Sleepers Initiative (a Government subsidy)
1992   £38 million
1993   £33 million

Nightline, a freephone out-of-hours telephone advice service for people with housing problems in London, was established by the charity Shelter in November 1991; it answered 23,000 calls in its first year

Newcastle
South Shields
Middlesborough
Irish Sea
Preston
Bradford
Leeds
Hull
North Sea
Bolton
Salford
Newton-le-Willows
Manchester
Warrington
Widnes
Sheffield
Kidsgrove
Stoke-on-Trent
Derby
Nottingham
Tamworth
Leicester
Birmingham
Rugby
Bedford
Milton Keynes
Luton
Hemel Hempstead
Chelmsford
London
Bristol
Bristol Channel
Leatherhead
Hove
Brighton
Plymouth
English Channel

0   kilometres   100
0   miles   60

© Martin Gilbert, 1993

133

PRIVATE CHARITY AND PUBLIC WELFARE

The work of several hundred individual charities in Britain makes a considerable contribution to health care and welfare. This map shows the Homes established by one such charity, the Sue Ryder Foundation. Sue Ryder (Lady Ryder of Warsaw) has established centres throughout the world, where the sick and the hungry can be helped. In Britain, more than 500 Sue Ryder shops sell goods to raise funds for her organisation's work

In the twelve-month period ending on 30 June 1992, a total of 2,342 patients were nursed in Sue Ryder Homes. In addition, 3,053 domiciliary visits were made, and 693 bereavement visits. A further 3,318 visits were made by patients to Day Centres

Ecclesmachan
various handicaps
24 beds

Greenlaw
various disabilities
40 beds

Temple Sowerby
disabled and elderly
23 beds

● Sue Ryder homes established
1953-1992
○ Sue Ryder homes in
preparation

Bamber Bridge
chronic sick &
physically handicapped
41 beds

Oxenhope
cancer patients
18 beds

Leeds
cancer patients
22 beds

Holme-upon-Spalding
physically disabled
47 beds

Billinge
elderly disabled
& frail
28 beds

Doncaster
physically handicapped
53 beds

Sheffield
discharged psychiatric patients
13 beds

Nottingham ○
being prepared

Snettisham
disabled and elderly
29 beds

Walsingham
a retreat house:
in one year, 3,611
people stayed

Ashby-de-la-Zouch
cancer patients
28 beds

Peterborough
cancer care & chronic sick
40 beds

Yeaton Peverey ○
being prepared

Ely
varying disabilities
40 beds

Moggerhanger
cancer patients
20 beds

Cavendish
physically
handicapped
30 beds

Cheltenham
cancer patients
25 beds

St Paul's Walden
physically handicapped
55 beds

Chantry Park
being prepared

Nettlebed
cancer patients
25 beds

Langrish
cancer patients
22 beds

0 kilometres 100

0 miles 60

© Martin Gilbert, 1993

"John Major has ordered a study of ways to increase the role of voluntary groups, charities and the private sector in easing the problems of the sick, needy and homeless", *The Times*, 1 January 1993

NEW UNIVERSITIES 1992–1993

The Higher and Further Education Act 1992 marked the end of the distinction between higher education provided by universities, and that provided by the polytechnics and colleges of higher education. Under the 1992 Act, polytechnics and colleges of higher education were permitted to apply to change their status to that of universities. The 32 that did so at the time of the passing of the Act are shown here. This raised the number of universities from 46 to 78

● Polytechnics and Colleges of Higher Education, changing their status to that of Universities in 1992-1993. The University names by which they have chosen to be known are given in capital letters

Aberdeen
ROBERT GORDON

Glasgow
QUEENS
Paisley
PAISLEY

Edinburgh
NAPIER

Newcastle
NORTHUMBRIA

Sunderland
SUNDERLAND

Middlesborough
TEESSIDE

Leeds
LEEDS METROPOLITAN

Hull
HUMBERSIDE

Preston
CENTRAL LANCASHIRE

Huddersfield
HUDDERSFIELD

Liverpool
JOHN MOORES

Manchester
MANCHESTER METROPOLITIAN

Stoke-on-Trent
STAFFORDSHIRE

Nottingham
NOTTINGHAM TRENT

Birmingham
CENTRAL ENGLAND

Coventry
COVENTRY

Leicester
DE MONTFORT

Chelmsford
ANGLIA POLYTECHNIC UNIVERSITY

Holloway Road
NORTH LONDON

White Hart Lane
MIDDLESEX

Hatfield
HERTFORDSHIRE

Pontypridd
GLAMORGAN

Ealing
THAMES VALLEY

Romford
EAST LONDON

Kingston-on-Thames
KINGSTON

Woolwich
GREENWICH

Borough Road
SOUTH BANK

Brighton
BRIGHTON

Fern Barrow
BOURNEMOUTH

Portsmouth
PORTSMOUTH

Plymouth
PLYMOUTH

0   kilometres   100

0   miles   60

In 1989-90 there were 689,100 students receiving higher education, of whom 79,500 were non-residential students at the Open University and 72,800 were from overseas. Adult education centres had an enrolment in 1989-90 of 1,586,000 students

© Martin Gilbert, 1993

135

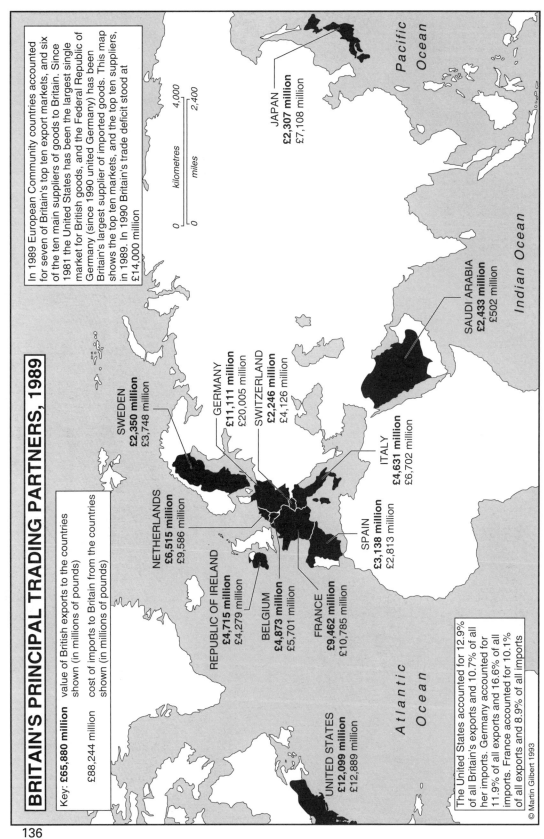

BRITAIN'S PRINCIPAL TRADING PARTNERS, 1989

Key: **£65,880 million**   value of British exports to the countries
shown (in millions of pounds)

£88,244 million   cost of imports to Britain from the countries
shown (in millions of pounds)

In 1989 European Community countries accounted for seven of Britain's top ten export markets, and six of the ten main suppliers of goods to Britain. Since 1981 the United States has been the largest single market for British goods, and the Federal Republic of Germany (since 1990 united Germany) has been Britain's largest supplier of imported goods. This map shows the top ten markets, and the top ten suppliers, in 1989. In 1990 Britain's trade deficit stood at £14,000 million

kilometres   4,000
miles   2,400

0

UNITED STATES
£12,099 million
£12,889 million

SWEDEN
£2,350 million
£3,748 million

GERMANY
£11,111 million
£20,005 million

SWITZERLAND
£2,246 million
£4,126 million

NETHERLANDS
£6,515 million
£9,586 million

REPUBLIC OF IRELAND
£4,715 million
£4,279 million

BELGIUM
£4,873 million
£5,701 million

FRANCE
£9,462 million
£10,785 million

SPAIN
£3,138 million
£2,813 million

ITALY
£4,631 million
£6,702 million

JAPAN
£2,307 million
£7,108 million

SAUDI ARABIA
£2,433 million
£502 million

Pacific Ocean

Indian Ocean

Atlantic Ocean

The United States accounted for 12.9% of all Britain's exports and 10.7% of all her imports. Germany accounted for 11.9% of all exports and 16.6% of all imports. France accounted for 10.1% of all exports and 8.9% of all imports

© Martin Gilbert 1993

BRITISH OVERSEAS DEPENDENT TERRITORIES, 1993

On 1 January 1993 there were fourteen British dependent territories, the last remnants of an Empire on which "the sun never set". Their total population was six million. The most populous, Hong Kong, with a population of 5,800,000, is to revert to China on 1 July 1997

The date shows the first year of British rule, the figure in black gives the population in 1992

HONG KONG
ceded, 1842
New Territories leased, 1898
5,800,000

DIEGO GARCIA

BRITISH INDIAN OCEAN TERRITORY
1965
no permanent inhabitants

On the expiry of the New Territories 99-year lease on 1 July 1997, both the New Territories leased in 1898 and the main island ceded to Britain by the Treaty of Nanking in 1842 will (under the Anglo-Chinese Joint Declaration of 27 May 1985) become a Special Administrative Region (SAR) of the People's Republic of China. The Declaration also states that the social and economic systems in the SAR will remain unchanged for a further fifty years

In October 1961, following the eruption of a volcano believed to have been extinct for thousands of years, the population of Tristan da Cunha was evacuated to Britain. They returned two years later

Mediterranean

3,316 merchant ships (totalling 61 million gross tons) entered the port in 1991

GIBRALTAR
1713
31,265

North Atlantic

TURKS & CAICOS ISLANDS
1765
14,000

CAYMAN ISLANDS
1734
27,000

BERMUDA
1609
60,000

BRITISH VIRGIN ISLANDS
1672
13,000

ANGUILLA
1650
8,800

MONTSERRAT
1783
13,000

ST HELENA
1834
5,644

ASCENSION
1815
1,129

South Atlantic

TRISTAN DA CUNHA
NIGHTINGALE ISLANDS
GOUGH ISLANDS
1816
288

SOUTH GEORGIA & SOUTH SANDWICH ISLANDS
1775
no permanent inhabitants

The population consists of an army unit and a civilian harbour master at King Edward Point, and the staff of the British Antarctic Survey at Bird Island

BIRD ISLAND
SOUTH ORKNEY

Pacific Ocean

PITCAIRN ISLANDS
PITCAIRN, HENDERSON, DUCIE, OENO
1887
56

FALKLAND ISLANDS
1833
2,000

BRITISH ANTARCTIC TERRITORY
1962
no permanent inhabitants

SOUTH SHETLAND
PALMER

© Martin Gilbert, 1993

137

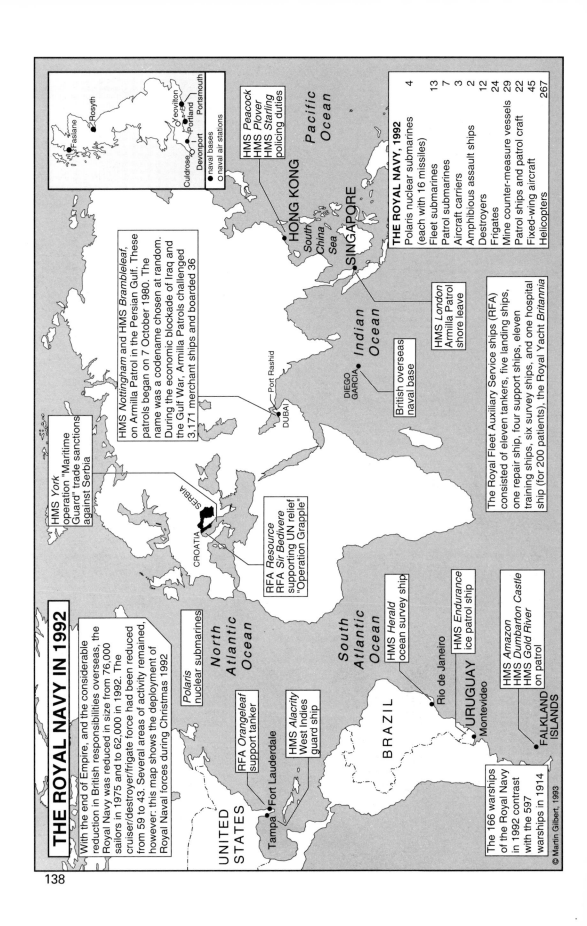

THE ROYAL NAVY IN 1992

With the end of Empire, and the considerable reduction in British responsibilities overseas, the Royal Navy was reduced in size from 76,000 sailors in 1975 and to 62,000 in 1992. The cruiser/destroyer/frigate force had been reduced from 59 to 43. Several areas of activity remained, however: this map shows the deployment of Royal Naval forces during Christmas 1992

HMS *York*
operation "Maritime Guard" trade sanctions against Serbia

HMS *Nottingham* and HMS *Brambleleaf*, on Armilla Patrol in the Persian Gulf. These patrols began on 7 October 1980. The name was a codename chosen at random. During the economic blockade of Iraq and the Gulf War, Armilla Patrols challenged 3,171 merchant ships and boarded 36

HMS *Peacock*
HMS *Plover*
HMS *Starling*
policing duties

HMS *London*
Armilla Patrol
shore leave

British overseas
naval base

RFA *Resource*
RFA *Sir Bedivere*
supporting UN relief
"Operation Grapple"

The Royal Fleet Auxiliary Service ships (RFA) consisted of eleven tankers, five landing ships, one repair ship, four support ships, eleven training ships, six survey ships, and one hospital ship (for 200 patients), the Royal Yacht *Britannia*

Polaris
nuclear submarines

RFA *Orangeleaf*
support tanker

HMS *Alacrity*
West Indies
guard ship

HMS *Herald*
ocean survey ship

HMS *Endurance*
ice patrol ship

HMS *Amazon*
HMS *Dumbarton Castle*
HMS *Gold River*
on patrol

The 166 warships
of the Royal Navy
in 1992 contrast
with the 597
warships in 1914

THE ROYAL NAVY, 1992	
Polaris nuclear submarines (each with 16 missiles)	4
Fleet submarines	13
Patrol submarines	7
Aircraft carriers	3
Amphibious assault ships	2
Destroyers	12
Frigates	24
Mine counter-measure vessels	29
Patrol ships and patrol craft	22
Fixed-wing aircraft	45
Helicopters	267

Pacific Ocean

South China Sea

HONG KONG

SINGAPORE

Indian Ocean

DIEGO GARCIA

Port Rashid

DUBAI

SERBIA

CROATIA

North Atlantic Ocean

South Atlantic Ocean

UNITED STATES

Tampa
Fort Lauderdale

BRAZIL

Rio de Janeiro

URUGUAY
Montevideo

FALKLAND ISLANDS

Faslane
Rosyth

Culdrose
Devonport
Portland
Portsmouth
Yeovilton

● naval bases
○ naval air stations

© Martin Gilbert, 1993

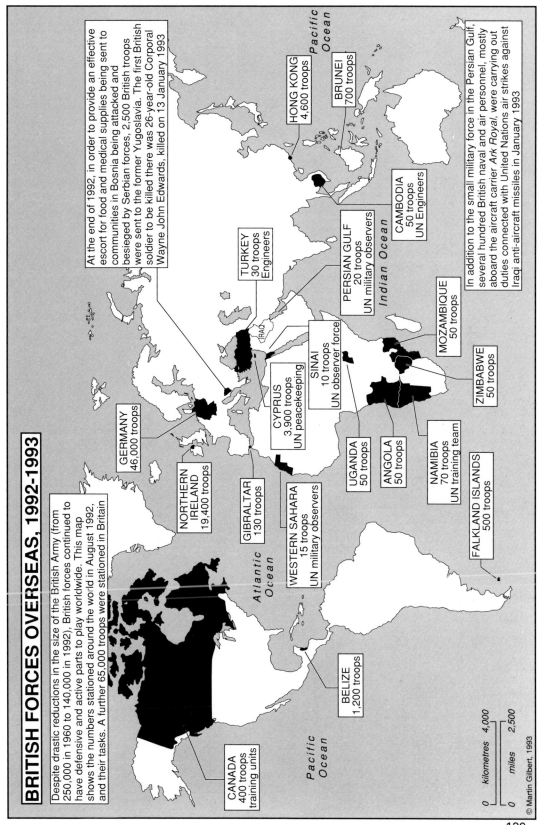

BRITISH FORCES OVERSEAS, 1992-1993

Despite drastic reductions in the size of the British Army (from 250,000 in 1960 to 140,000 in 1992), British forces continued to have defensive and active parts to play worldwide. This map shows the numbers stationed around the world in August 1992, and their tasks. A further 65,000 troops were stationed in Britain

At the end of 1992, in order to provide an effective escort for food and medical supplies being sent to communities in Bosnia being attacked and besieged by Serbian forces, 2,500 British troops were sent to the former Yugoslavia. The first British soldier to be killed there was 26-year-old Corporal Wayne John Edwards, killed on 13 January 1993

In addition to the small military force in the Persian Gulf, several hundred British naval and air personnel, mostly aboard the aircraft carrier *Ark Royal*, were carrying out duties connected with United Nations air strikes against Iraqi anti-aircraft missiles in January 1993

HONG KONG
4,600 troops

BRUNEI
700 troops

CAMBODIA
50 troops
UN Engineers

TURKEY
30 troops
Engineers

PERSIAN GULF
20 troops
UN military observers

MOZAMBIQUE
50 troops

ZIMBABWE
50 troops

SINAI
10 troops
UN observer force

CYPRUS
3,900 troops
UN peacekeeping

GERMANY
46,000 troops

NORTHERN
IRELAND
19,400 troops

GIBRALTAR
130 troops

WESTERN SAHARA
15 troops
UN military observers

UGANDA
50 troops

ANGOLA
50 troops

NAMIBIA
70 troops
UN training team

FALKLAND ISLANDS
500 troops

BELIZE
1,200 troops

CANADA
400 troops
training units

IRAQ

*Pacific
Ocean*

*Atlantic
Ocean*

*Pacific
Ocean*

Indian Ocean

0   kilometres   4,000
0   miles   2,500

© Martin Gilbert, 1993

139

TOWARDS A SINGLE EUROPEAN MARKET, OCTOBER-DECEMBER 1992

The Maastricht Treaty of 7 February 1992 committed the European Community to a future common foreign and defence policy and a single currency. On June 2, Denmark voted by referendum against ratifying the Treaty (50.7% against). On September 16, after two months of currency crisis, Britain, then holding the Presidency of the European Community, withdrew from the Exchange Rate Mechanism (ERM). Between October and December 1992 the British Prime Minister, John Major, made the journeys shown here to repair divisions in the Community in preparation for the Edinburgh Summit

It was agreed at the Edinburgh Summit to co-ordinate aid and peace monitors for the former Yugoslav province of Macedonia, and to give £1,600 million for economic reconstruction in Poland, Hungary and Czechoslovakia (which became two States, the Czech Republic and Slovakia, on 1 January 1993)

Agreements at Edinburgh included authorisation of negotiations to bring Sweden, Finland and Austria into the European Community; and to prepare Poland and Hungary for membership. It was agreed that national decisions should be the rule, and action by Brussels the exception ("subsidiarity"). Community debates were to be opened up, voting records published, and legislation simplified

"I believe that the majority of people in this country want us to make a success of our membership of the European Community. This is not just a matter of idealism, it is a matter of hard-headed national self-interest" John Major, 14 December 1992

① London 28 October
② Birmingham 16 October
③ Brussels 23 November
④ Rome 27 November
⑤ Athens 28 November
⑥ Luxembourg 30 November
⑦ Madrid 30 November
⑧ Lisbon 1 December
⑨ Copenhagen 2 December
⑩ The Hague 6 December
⑪ Dublin 10 December
⑫ Edinburgh 11-12 December
⑬ Strasbourg 16 December
⑭ Ottawa 17 December
⑮ Washington 18 December

FINLAND

NORWAY

SWEDEN

DENMARK

Baltic Sea

POLAND

North Sea

NETHERLANDS

BELGIUM

EIRE

GERMANY

CZECH REPUBLIC

SLOVAKIA

AUSTRIA

HUNGARY

SWITZERLAND

SLOVENIA

CROATIA

BOSNIA

SERBIA

MACEDONIA

FRANCE

English Channel

Bay of Biscay

SPAIN

PORTUGAL

Atlantic Ocean

ITALY

Adriatic Sea

Mediterranean Sea

Aegean Sea

Black Sea

0   kilometres   400
0   miles   300

© Martin Gilbert, 1993

140

A PRIME MINISTER'S JOURNEYS, 1990-1993

Between becoming Prime Minister in November 1990, and the end of January 1993, John Major made 42 journeys overseas, 14 of them beyond Western Europe. The first, in December 1990, was to Rome, the forty-second, in January 1993, to India, Oman and Saudi Arabia. Further visits planned for 1993 included Switzerland and Tokyo

❶ 13-15 December 1990	⑯ 14-22 October 1991
❷ 20-22 December 1990	⑰ 6-8 November 1991
❸ 6-9 January 1991	⑱ 10 November 1991
❹ 14 January 1991	⑲ 27 November 1991
❺ 11 February 1991	⑳ 27 November 1991
❻ 4-6 March 1991	㉑ 4 December 1991
❼ 15-17 March 1991	㉒ 9-10 December 1991
❽ 8 April 1991	㉓ 25-26 May 1992
❾ 24 June 1991	㉔ 8 June 1992
❿ 27-29 June 1991	㉕ 6-13 June 1992
⑪ 2-13 August 1991	㉖ 6-13 June 1992
⑫ 27-30 August 1991	㉗ 26-27 June 1992
⑬ 1-8 September 1991	㉘ 6-8 July 1992
⑭ 11 September 1991	㉙ 9-11 July 1992
⑮ 18 September 1991	㉚ 7-9 August 1992
㉛ 30 September 1992	
㉜ 23-25 October 1992	
㉝ 23 November 1992	
㉞ 27-28 November '92	
㉟ 30 Nov.-1 Dec. 1992	
㊱ 2 December 1992	
㊲ 6 December 1992	
㊳ 7 December 1992	
㊴ 16 December 1992	
㊵ 17-21 December '92	
㊶ 22 December 1992	
㊷ 23-28 January 1993	
㊸ 23-25 February 1993	
㊹ spring 1993	
㊺ July 1993	

© Martin Gilbert, 1993

THE LONG-TERM UNEMPLOYED, 1993

At the beginning of 1993 the number of unemployed people in Britain rose to almost three million. Of these, a million were long-term unemployed, those who had not been in work for a year or more. This map shows the numbers of long-term unemployed region-by-region on 1 January 1993. Between 1 January and 11 March 1993, a further 100,000 job losses were announced

UNEMPLOYMENT
IN THE UNITED KINGDOM
January 1993: 2,993,000
February 1993: 2,971,000

long-term unemployed, on 1 January 1993 (total 1,030,020)

some regional job losses announced in December 1992 and in January and February 1993, to take effect in 1993

On 13 October 1992 it was announced that fifty coal mines would be closed, with the loss of 30,000 jobs. Following widespread public concern, the Government reduced the number of pit closures to thirty, bringing the job losses to less than 20,000

On 11 March 1993 Rolls Royce announced the loss over the next two years of 5,000 jobs, mostly in Derby

The money paid out by the Government for unemployment benefit in 1992-1993 was £9,300 million. Job Centres, Job Clubs and Job Training Schemes were in existence since the mid-1980s to try to find work, or to provide work skills, for the unemployed

In three of the regions, East Anglia, the South East, and the South West, the number of long-term unemployed had doubled within twelve months

SCOTLAND 85,300

NORTHERN IRELAND 56,100

NORTH 59,900

Rosyth 550

LANCASHIRE 574

YORKSHIRE & HUMBERSIDE 88,100

Leeds 500

NORTH WEST 122,600

Halewood 470

EAST MIDLANDS 62,800

Derby 5,000

WEST MIDLANDS 106,800

WALES 46,000

EAST ANGLIA 24,700

SOUTH EAST & GREATER LONDON 307,300

Woodford 600

London 3,200

Rochester 510

Dagenham 660

Filton 650

SOUTH WEST 70,600

0 kilometres 100
0 miles 60

© Martin Gilbert 1993

142

MUSLIMS, SIKHS, HINDUS, JEWS AND BUDDHISTS, 1993

With the growth of immigration after the Second World War, considerable Muslim, Sikh and Hindu communities were established in Britain. Several thousand survivors of the Holocaust added to the already large Jewish communitiy. This map shows the main minority religious communities in 1993

In 1987 the Inter-Faith Network for the UK was established, linking the Christian and non-Christian communities. "This movement is dedicated to the celebration of differences, rather than viewing them as problems. The presence of these communities in Britain has enriched the fabric of society, and illustrates Britain's ability to welcome and integrate productive newcomers". (Rabbi Hugo Gryn, Holocaust survivor and founding co-chair of the Inter-Faith Network, 31 January 1993)

● main Muslim centres
◉ main Sikh centres
◒ main Hindu centres
● main Jewish centres
▲ Buddhist temples and monasteries

MINORITY RELIGIOUS COMMUNITIES, 1993

Muslims	1-2 million (300 mosques)
Sikhs	400,000 (175 gurdwaras)
Hindus	350,000 (150 temples)
Jews	300,000 (356 synagogues)
Buddhists	25,000 (50 temples & monasteries)

Glasgow   Edinburgh

Eskdale Muir

Belsay
Hexham
Gateshead

Ulverston

Pocklington

Bradford   Leeds
Billinge   Huddersfield
Liverpool   Manchester
Chorton-cum-Hardy   Buxton

Nottingham

Handsworth
Birmingham   Loughborough   East Dereham
Wolverhampton
Dudley   Leicester
Coventry

Milton Keynes
Lower Fulbrook   Watford   Radlett
Raglan   Great Gaddesden   Westcliffe
Cardiff   Bourne End   London   Southend
Reading   Kingston   Selsdon   Ilford
Christhurst
Southampton
Upottery   Bournemouth   Hove   Brighton

1993, the centenary of the 1893 Chicago World's Parliament of Religions, was designated Year of Religious Understanding and Co-operation. Multi-faith meetings, and prayer gatherings world-wide, culminated in a peace march on Parliament Hill, London, on Good Friday, 9 April 1993

0   kilometres   100
0   miles   60

© Martin Gilbert, 1993

PUBLIC SPENDING, 1993-1994

Total Government spending for the fiscal year 1993-1994 has been set at £243.8 billion. The previous fiscal year had been £256.3 billion. The amount shown in bold figures on this map is the departmental share of total government spending allocated for 1993-1994. The figure in italics indicates its percentage of the total

A Downing Street directive of 1991 stated: "The Government agreed that strict control of public spending...must be maintained by sticking as closely as possible to existing planning totals, with the aim of keeping the ratio of public spending...on a downward trend"

Under an agreement reached with King George III in 1760, all revenue from the Crown Estates goes to the Government, in return for a Civil List payment to the sovereign. In 1990, £70 million was received by the Government from the Crown Estates. In 1993 the Queen will receive £7,600,000 (.005% of Government spending) under the Civil List, but will pay £6,600,000 of this for the support of other members of the Royal Family. From 6 April 1993 she will also pay income tax

SCOTLAND
£13.86 billion
5.6%

DEFENCE
£23.52 billion
9.64%

NORTHERN IRELAND
£4.8 billion
2%

EDUCATION
£9.52 billion
3.90%

WALES
£7.2 billion
3%

LOCAL GOVERNMENT
£24.22 billion
9.93%

HEALTH
£29.88 billion
12.25%

NATIONAL HERITAGE
£0.99 billion
0.4%

TRANSPORT
£6.43 billion
2.63%

EMPLOYMENT
£3.74 billion
1.53%

TRADE & INDUSTRY
£2.59 billion
1.06%

AGRICULTURE
£2.59 billion
1.06%

FOREIGN & OVERSEAS
£3.49 billion
1.43%

SOCIAL SECURITY
£65 billion
26.66%

ENVIRONMENT
£38.82 billion
15.92%

HOME OFFICE
£6.12 billion
2.51%

The largest block of Government spending since 1945 has been Social Security, including the payment of unemployment and other benefits (in 1993) for 3 million unemployed. Social Security accounts for more than a quarter of all spending. Unemployment benefit totalled £9,300 million in 1992-3

The excess of Government spending over income for the year 1993-1994 estimated at £31.1 billion. On 1 January 1993 the Government deficit, the National Debt, stood at just over £200 billion. Of this, £16.5 billion were paid in debt interest in 1992-3. Britain's contribution to the European Community for the fiscal year 1992-93 was £2.46 billion